ROME BABYLON THE GREAT AND EUROPE

© BOB MITCHELL 2003

DEDICATION

This book is dedicated to the memory of those heroes of the Christian faith who knew their Bible, stood against the teachings of Rome and as a result gave their lives to preserve freedom of speech and the undiluted Gospel of Jesus Christ for future generations.

It is also dedicated to those gallant men and women who, in past wars, so willingly made the supreme sacrifice in order to preserve the freedom we are blessed to enjoy today. A freedom so many are foolishly offering on the altar of a New Roman Empire.

Also, it is an honour to dedicate this book to the loving memory of that exciting teacher on Bible prophecy, Barry Smith of New Zealand. Barry went home to be with the Lord on June 26 2002. It was following a meeting in Kent, England in the late 1980's that Barry encouraged the author to go out and preach on the Second Coming of the Lord Jesus Christ.

May God continue to bless Barry's ministry through his books and tapes we are privileged to still have with us. Though dead yet he speaks. I am sure the first words Barry heard in Heaven were "Well done thou good and faithful servant."

May we follow the example of Barry and his family in preaching the end time message for as long as we are able.

I cannot help but dedicate this volume to my dearest Maria. Thank you for your prayers, patience, encouragement, love and incredible generosity far and above all I could have asked. Why God should bless me with such a special wife will, forever, be a complete yet wonderful mystery to me. Your deep spirituality is a constant challenge to my own walk with the Lord. Your totally crazy sense of humour chases away all clouds. You are of more value than many, many rubies.

To my darling daughters. Each of you are so very special to me. God has truly blessed me with you all. Any Father would be pleased to call you his. But I am so very proud to know you are my very own. I love you so very much.

To the many friends around Britain who have invited me to speak on Bible prophecy and who, unknown to them, the Lord used to supply me with information and anecdotes I was seeking at the time. Your love and friendship are greatly valued. I must mention Rose and Terry Miller who have been a constant source of encouragement and blessing to Maria and myself not least because it was they who introduced us to one another. You bring us very fond memories of love, laughter, rich conversation and excellent food. May the Lord richly reward your efforts as you sound the alarm. All of you are lights in an ever darkening world.

Finally above all, I thank the Lord Jesus Christ. My Saviour, Master and closest, never failing, friend who has shown such mercy to me over the last 40 years that I have been privileged to know Him. May all who read the following pages follow and dedicate their lives to the service of this Wonderful One.

JESUS CHRIST, MESSIAH OF ISRAEL, LORD OF THE CHURCH, THE SAVIOUR OF THE WORLD AND SOON RETURNING KING.

Bob Mitchell, England, January 2003

CONTENTS

INTRODUCTION
8

CHAPTER I
KING NEBUCHADNEZZAR'S DREAM
17

CHAPTER II
THE DREAM OF REVIVED ROME
37

CHAPTER III
THE VATICAN, POLITICS AND WAR
44

CHAPTER IV
THE VATICAN RAT LINES AND THE NUREMBERG TRIALS
68

CHAPTER V
THE BIRTH OF AN EMPIRE
76

CHAPTER VI
MYSTERY BABYLON THE GREAT
93

CHAPTER VII
BABYLON COMES TO ROME
125

CHAPTER VIII
ALL ROADS LEAD TO ROME
135

CHAPTER IX
THE WHORE AND HER LOVERS
147

CHAPTER X
MARY, MOTHER GODDESS OF THE NEW WORLD RELIGION
169

CHAPTER XI
THE VATICAN AND THE POLITICS OF THE NEW WORLD ORDER
191

CHAPTER XII
THE SYMBOLISM OF ROME, BABYLON AND REVELATION IN THE E.U.
213

CHAPTER XIII
THE GREAT FALLING AWAY
224

CHAPTER XIV
THE STARS ARE FALLING BUT THE SON WILL SOON ARISE
235

REFERENCES:
364

ROME, BABYLON THE GREAT AND EUROPE

INTRODUCTION

The days in which you and I find ourselves are without doubt the most amazing days in the history of the planet. World events assail our eyes and ears with such rapidity it would have made our Grandparents heads spin. We are barely able to assimilate and prioritise the vast amount of information with which we are constantly bombarded. Technology has exploded before our eyes providing us with, among other things, the ability to communicate with the other side of the planet in an instant, whereas just a few short years ago it would have taken weeks to hear from our loved ones abroad. When the Pilgrim Fathers set sail for the Americas in the 17th century it took them 3 months to sail across the life threatening Atlantic Ocean to reach their promised land. Today I am able to have breakfast at home in England and my lunch in the United States. In less than 100 years we have travelled from the horse to the car to the airplane to the spaceship. Such a gigantic leap is unparalleled in history. Computer science is moving forward at such a speed that newly built computers are out of date almost as soon as they leave the factory. As they are loaded onto the transport bringing them to your town, new technology is being added to the computers being manufactured on the production line behind them.
We now have computers fitted with brain cells in the

hope they will eventually be able to think for themselves. Frighteningly, at the same time, weapons of such devastating destructive power are being invented almost daily. Biological weapons so potent they could literally wipe the human race out of existence within days if not hours. For instance, by 2004 if not earlier, many, what the West would call, "unstable" nations will have developed their own weapons of mass destruction ready to unleash them on their enemies. The 21st century promises an explosion of knowledge and technological advancement totally beyond the dreams of our recent ancestors. In such a world where science fiction becomes science fact and either Utopia or extinction seem to be around the next corner, many voices are being heard calling for a central World Government. One that can oversee and control the planet. A government under which we and our children will be provided with the Utopian peace we all desire. In a world where all men are able to sleep at night in peace and safety. Who will come and grant us the peace we all desire?

To those who believe the Bible has absolutely nothing to say to the man or woman of the 21st century, it comes as a huge shock to discover that these are the very days about which these ancient Hebrew scriptures have much to say indeed. We are passing through a unique period in human history. An incredible period when we are seeing biblical prophecies uttered thousands of years ago, springing to life before our eyes. Yet amazingly, sadly, people would rather trust their local medium or read the so-called "prophecies" of Nostradamus, written in such vague poetic verse that they could mean almost anything. Despite the same charge of "meaning anything" being levelled at the prophecies of the Bible, when one actually looks at them instead of simply listening to the opinions of others, one is amazed at the intricate and very detailed way many of the prophecies are written. The accusation, that they can be interpreted according to ones own preferences, has no basis. Such a charge is unfounded. We neglect the reading of these ancient Hebrew prophecies at our peril, because to read them and take them on board is to forewarn and prepare ourselves for what is about to happen.

The Last Days

The ancient scriptures speak of a coming period in history known as the "last days" or the "end times" when a World Government will arise. It will be ruled by a man the Bible calls the Antichrist (1 John 2:18) or the beast (Rev. 13) to name just two of his biblical titles though of course his actual name is at this time unknown to us. For reasons that shall become evident as you continue reading, students of Bible prophecy have given this coming World Government the title "Revived Roman Empire." This empire although having its birth in Europe will eventually rule the entire planet.

Alongside the Antichrist will be a religious leader known in biblical terms as the "second beast" (Rev. 13:11-18). He is also referred to as the "false prophet" (Rev. 19:20) who will cause all the earth to worship the Antichrist (Rev. 13:14,15).

At the same time a false world religious system based

mainly in Rome (Rev. 17) will ride and direct the kingdom of the Antichrist. As we continue we shall explain just why Rome figures so prominently in our study. The exact connection the false religious leader and the Antichrist have with the prophesied false religion based in Rome is something students of prophecy have discussed for centuries. Fulfilled prophecy, in the near future, will make all things clear.

In this present book we shall be looking at the religion presently based in Rome, the Roman Catholic Church. Also, we shall look at the history of Roman Catholicism and its role, past and present, in shaping the destiny of Europe, the grave of the old Roman Empire.

Furthermore this book will uncover the Catholic Church's political as well as spiritual goals. I believe Rome has a plan for you and I, which reveals her as the prophesied false religion of Revelation 17. She will be the woman who rides the Revived Roman Empire under Antichrist as seen in Revelation 17. She will grow bolder yet. She will grow into a great world wide "Church" encompassing, most beliefs under her wing apart from the true faith revealed in the Bible. The faith, which believes Jesus Christ alone, is the way to salvation and eternal life. Not Islam, Buddhism or any other faith but the faith in Jesus the Messiah of Israel and the world as revealed in the Bible. Even many of those professing to follow the Lord Jesus will be swept along in the euphoria of this seemingly beneficent, all embracing, "all paths lead to God" religion.

Also I shall endeavour to show that the Roman Catholic Church is opposed to biblical Christianity.

What I mean by "biblical Christianity" is the belief that the Bible *alone* is the inspired, infallible word of God. That Jesus Christ is the *only* way to God. That man can have peace with God through faith in Jesus Christ alone, without having to obey Church rules and traditions in order to find acceptance and peace with the Almighty.

The Roman Catholic Church lays down rules and regulations to be obeyed in order to get to Heaven.
Rules and observances found nowhere in the Bible. To the Catholic mind, failure to observe even one of these rules may result in damnation. I am so glad to inform you they are wrong. The Bible is clear. You can find peace with God without the millstone of Rome's regulations being hung around your neck. In fact the rules of Rome will lead you away from peace with God and cause you to walk a treadmill of man made observances that bring no real peace, only self satisfaction or outright condemnation. Satisfaction in the misguided belief you are working your way to Heaven or condemnation as you rightly realise you will never be good enough for a Holy God. Jesus came to set you free from both. We shall explain this, also, as we go along.

Without being patronising, let me also state, I am certain many Roman Catholics have a true relationship with the Lord Jesus. They believe that Jesus' death and his death alone cleansed their sins when he died on the cross of Calvary 2,000 years ago.

They believe there is nothing more that can be done to save them. Through disregarding the rules and observances Rome believes are necessary for salvation, these believers are in fact no longer strictly Roman Catholics. They merely attend Catholic Churches.

Jesus, who was in fact God in the flesh, shouted in triumph, as he died on a Roman cross, *"It is finished"* (John 19:30). The price for our redemption was paid in full. No amount of good deeds, penance, graces from Mary, walking on my knees for Mary or anyone else, prayers for the dead or any work of my own hands will alter or add to, the finished work of the Lord Jesus. God paid for my sins by coming and dying once and for all in my place (Heb. 9:28; 10:10-14). The believers within the Roman Catholic religion are attempting to work from the inside out. They are hoping, praying and working to change the Catholic Church from within. To make known the true Gospel of the Lord Jesus as revealed in the scriptures and not the Gospel of salvation through works promoted by Rome.

I have to say, with the greatest respect, I do not think that will happen. But as Rome grows ever more ecumenical they may eventually be forced to leave the Catholic Church. I believe the word of God speaks very clearly to the believers seeking to change Rome from within. In fact it is also a word to all believers who are involved in the very questionable moves toward unity within the Ecumenical and Charismatic movements, *"Come out of her my people"* (Rev.18:4).

Notice, God says "My people". He does not say they are not his. He says they are His very own possession. But He warns them, do not partake in her sins or you will be partakers in the judgement that is coming. Come out of her now.

As we journey through this book we shall be looking at some of the teachings of the Roman Catholic Church. We shall also be seeking to understand the goals of those powerful people who operate in front of and behind the scenes within the Catholic Church itself, within the Charismatic and Ecumenical Movements and within the United Nations and European Union's halls of power.

Let me also state I am not writing with the intention of being controversial. However, because of its content, the present volume cannot help but be so. Also, please allow me to say I have no axe to grind against sincere Catholic people. I would agree there is much wrong in Protestantism. There is a lot wrong in many branches of Evangelicalism.

Within Pentecostalism. Certainly within the Charismatic movement there is much we could point to as being wrong. This book will touch only on those points as they relate to the present study. But when the Bible speaks of the coming false World Religion riding and directing the coming World Government I believe it is speaking about the Roman Catholic Church and a World Religion into which she will yet evolve.

Much of the professing Christian Church has been tricked. They have swallowed a lie. A lie that says Rome has changed from the time of the Protestant Martyrs. Those heroes of the faith who were willing to be burned at the stake for declaring many of Rome's teachings to be anti-scriptural. Indeed Rome has not changed but continues to believe in and practice the very things the Martyrs stood against. This book will also endeavour to prove Rome has always had a plan to dominate Europe as she did in her earlier years following the demise of the Roman Empire.

As you read on you will be made aware, if you are not already, of the origin of many of the beliefs found in today's Roman Catholic Church. Her plans for the professing Christian Church and for other faiths. Her plans for Europe and the world. These plans will continue to bear fruit and grow until Rome is finally judged through the channels God chooses in the last days (Rev.18). This judgement will not be directed solely upon the Roman Catholicism we see today, but upon something I believe she is evolving into before our eyes. A "One World" religion willing to shelter all manner of birds within the branches of this coming Frankenstein monster of a "Church". But at the very heart of this coming World Religion will be the Roman Catholic religion and Rome.

Those days and the days of the Antichrist World Government are almost upon us.

Finally I do not claim to have a monopoly on truth. I could be wrong on some prophetic points within this volume. However I do believe the main core of the book to be substantially correct when gazing into the future the Bible predicts for planet Earth.

But before we fix our gaze upon these coming events, we must travel back into the past. Our journey begins in ancient Babylon, where the king is having a restless night............................

Chapter 1

KING NEBUCHADNEZZAR'S DREAM

Dan 2:1-13

1 And in the second year of the reign of Nebuchadnezzar Nebuchadnezzar dreamed dreams, wherewith his spirit was troubled, and his sleep brake from him.

2 Then the king commanded to call the magicians, and the astrologers, and the sorcerers, and the Chaldeans, for to shew the king his dreams. So they came and stood before the king.

3 And the king said unto them, I have dreamed a dream, and my spirit was troubled to know the dream.

4 Then spake the Chaldeans to the king in Syriack, O king, live for ever: tell thy servants the dream, and we will shew the interpretation.

5 The king answered and said to the Chaldeans, The thing is gone from me: if ye will not make known unto me the dream, with the interpretation thereof, ye shall be cut in pieces, and your houses shall be made a dunghill.

6 But if ye shew the dream, and the interpretation thereof, ye shall receive of me gifts and rewards and great honour: therefore shew me the dream, and the interpretation thereof.

7   They answered again and said, Let the king tell his servants the dream, and we will shew the interpretation of it.

8   The king answered and said, I know of certainty that ye would gain the time, because ye see the thing is gone from me.

9   But if ye will not make known unto me the dream, there is but one decree for you: for ye have prepared lying and corrupt words to speak before me, till the time be changed: therefore tell me the dream, and I shall know that ye can shew me the interpretation thereof.

10   The Chaldeans answered before the king, and said, There is not a man upon the earth that can shew the king's matter: therefore there is no king, lord, nor ruler, that asked such things at any magician, or astrologer, or Chaldean.

11   And it is a rare thing that the king requireth, and

there is none other that can shew it before the king, except the gods, whose dwelling is not with flesh.

12   For this cause the king was angry and very furious, and commanded to destroy all the wise men of Babylon.

13   And the decree went forth that the wise men should be slain; and they sought Daniel and his fellows to be slain.

   In Daniel chapter 2, King Nebuchadnezzar, king of Babylon, had a dream.
A dream which greatly disturbed him. To the horror

and trepidation of his psychics, astrologers, magicians and wise men, once the king awoke not only did he forget the dream but also he continued to be troubled by it. To their even greater consternation he commanded that if they could not tell him the dream and the interpretation they would be cut in pieces. How many modern day psychics and astrology gurus would step forward to take up such a challenge? Only Daniel, the captive, could tell the king exactly what he had seen in his dream and the interpretation thereof. Only Daniel, this young prince of the tribe of Judah, taken captive when Nebuchadnezzar's army laid siege to and captured the beloved holy city, Jerusalem. Only a man of God, inspired by the Spirit of God, would be able give the king the complete answer he longed to hear. Daniel was that man.

May all psychics and so called prophets take serious note. When a prophet of God prophesies, he is, all the time, 100% correct. If he is not, then according to Moses (Deut.18:22) he is a false prophet. God's pass mark for a true prophet is 100%. Not 60% or even 80% but 100%. It is an awesome responsibility to take to oneself the sacred title of prophet. There is no scriptural warranty for getting it right only some of the time and continuing to call yourself a true prophet.
A good guesser maybe. But definitely not a prophet of the God of Israel and the Church. If the prophets of the Bible were as wide of the mark as those who dare to call themselves prophets today, the entire prophetic utterances of the Bible would be called into question.
Leaving aside false cults such as Jehovah's Witnesses, Mormons etc., many so called Christian "prophets" are, by the above definition, false prophets. When the

predictions they have uttered prove false, they should have the courage and backbone to say they are wrong and take a back seat as far as prophesying is concerned. They bring shame upon the Church if they continue in the office of "prophet". It matters little, how much you say you love the Lord if you continue to rebel against his word. In Luke 6:46 Jesus asked, *"Why call ye me Lord, Lord and yet do not the things which I say?"* And in Matthew 7:21 in the middle of warning us to beware of false prophets, the Lord made the following sobering statement: *"Not everyone that saith unto me Lord, Lord, shall enter into the kingdom of Heaven; but he that doeth the will of my Father which is in Heaven"* And again in John 14:15 *"If ye love me keep my commandments."* If Jesus' commandments are in direct agreement with the Father they must agree with all scripture for *"all scripture is given by inspiration of God"* (1 Tim. 3:16). Therefore if you have prophesied falsely you are by definition a false prophet. There is no way around this. But here is good news, if you have prophesied and it has failed to come to pass, step back, confess your error and God will forgive you and bless you for your honesty.

If you support a known false prophet, you are supporting a person who has gone against the revealed word of God Himself. It is as simple and as serious as that. God will hold both you and them accountable. Just as true prophets and their listeners will receive a reward, false prophets will receive punishment from the Lord. And so will those who continue to follow and support them. Those who know full well what they predicted has not come to pass or that the doctrine they espouse is to be found nowhere in scripture. Yet if they wilfully continue to encourage these people in their error and recommend them to others they too will be judged alongside the False Prophets they have supported. This is very serious indeed and must not be passed over lightly. We are responsible to God himself. And it is to him alone we shall all individually, face to face, give an account. We point the finger at the false predictions of the Jehovah's Witnesses or the Mormons but are very loath to point out the False Prophets within our own ranks. Shame on us. When we behave in such a deceptive manner we are no better than those who continue to uphold the teachings of the false cults. But, back to Babylon and a true prophet, Daniel......

Dan 2:25-45

25 Then Arioch brought in Daniel before the king in haste, and said thus unto him, I have found a man of the captives of Judah, that will make known unto the king the interpretation.

26 The king answered and said to Daniel, whose name was Belteshazzar, Art thou able to make known unto me the dream which I have seen, and the interpretation thereof?

27 Daniel answered in the presence of the king, and said, The secret which the king hath demanded cannot the wise men, the astrologers, the magicians
the soothsayers, shew unto the king;

28 But there is a God in Heaven that revealeth secrets, and maketh known to the king Nebuchadnezzar what shall be in the latter days. Thy dream, and the visions of thy head upon thy bed, are these;

29 As for thee, O king, thy thoughts came into thy mind

upon thy bed, what should come to pass hereafter: and he that revealeth secrets maketh known to thee what shall come to pass.

30 But as for me, this secret is not revealed to me for any wisdom that I have more than any living, but for their sakes that shall make known the interpretation to the king, and that thou mightest know the thoughts of thy heart.

31 Thou, O king, sawest, and behold a great image. This great image, whose brightness was excellent, stood before thee; and the form thereof was terrible.

32 This image's head was of fine gold, his breast and his arms of silver, his belly and his thighs of brass,

33 His legs of iron, his feet part of iron and part of clay.

34 Thou sawest till that a stone was cut out without hands, which smote the image upon his feet that were of iron and clay, and brake them to pieces.

35 Then was the iron, the clay, the brass, the silver, and the gold, broken to pieces together, and became like the chaff of the summer threshingfloors; and the wind carried them away, that no place was found for them: and the stone that smote the image became a great mountain, and filled the whole earth.

36 This is the dream; and we will tell the interpretation thereof before the king.

37 Thou, O king, art a king of kings: for the God of Heaven hath given thee a kingdom, power, and strength, and glory.

38 And wheresoever the children of men dwell, the beasts of the

field and the fowls of the Heaven hath he given into thine hand, and hath made thee ruler over them all. Thou art this head of gold.

39 And after thee shall arise another kingdom inferior to thee, and another third kingdom of brass, which shall bear rule over all the earth.

40 And the fourth kingdom shall be strong as iron: forasmuch as iron breaketh in pieces and subdueth all things: and as iron that breaketh all these, shall it break in pieces and bruise.

41 And whereas thou sawest the feet and toes, part of potters' clay, and part of iron, the kingdom shall be divided; but there shall be in it of the strength of the iron, forasmuch as thou sawest the iron mixed with miry clay.

42 And as the toes of the feet were part of iron, and part of clay, so the kingdom shall be partly strong, and partly broken.

43 And whereas thou sawest iron mixed with miry clay, they shall mingle themselves with the seed of men: but they shall not cleave one to another, even as iron is not mixed with clay.

44 And in the days of these kings shall the God of Heaven set up a kingdom,
which shall never be destroyed: and the kingdom shall not be left to other people, but it shall break in pieces and consume all these kingdoms, and it shall stand for ever.

45 Forasmuch as thou sawest that the stone was cut out of the mountain without hands, and that it brake in pieces the iron, the brass, the clay, the silver, and the gold; the great God hath made known to the king what shall come to pass hereafter: and the

dream is certain, and the interpretation thereof sure.

As the king lay pondering his great empire and all the lands over which he held sway, he began to wonder what would happen after he had passed from this life (Dan. 2:28). He fell into a sleep and dreamed. Before him he saw a great statue of a man. The head was of gold; the chest was of silver; the belly and thighs were composed of bronze. The legs of the image were of iron and the feet were of iron mixed with clay. As Nebuchadnezzar watched in wonder, he witnessed a stone cut without hands strike the ten toes of the image. The entire edifice collapsed into dust and was blown away from his sight. The stone which had struck the image a deathblow suddenly grew into a mountain that filled the whole earth. What could it all mean? The interpretation Daniel gave to king Nebuchadnezzar concerning his dream was incredible! Unbelievable were it not for the fact that it is written here for all sceptics to gaze upon in wonder and confusion. For the dream was, in fact a message, recognised by students of Bible prophecy down the ages, as a run-down of five major world empires that would each rise and fall.

(1) THE HEAD OF GOLD
    BABYLON

(2) THE CHEST AND ARMS OF SILVER
    MEDO/PERSIA

(3) BELLY AND THIGHS OF BRONZE
    GREECE

(4) LEGS OF IRON
    ROME

(5) FEET AND TOES OF IRON AND CLAY
    REVIVED ROME

The prophet Daniel told king Nebuchadnezzar that in the coming days five empires would each rise and vanish into history before the Jewish Messiah appears to set up his own physical kingdom. He is the stone that will crush and destroy the fifth empire and set up his own kingdom on planet earth! This was the dream given to the king of ancient Babylon, recorded more than 2,500 years ago when only the first empire was visible. Please tell me, who, in their right mind, would spend their money and their hopes on the mystical, unclear writings of someone such as Nostradamus when this amazing Bible is before us? With its stupendous, mind numbing accuracy. The prophecies of the Bible are not written for us in mystical indiscernible verse. But in clear language. Their very fulfilment being verified by history and archaeology. Remember, this prophecy was written two and a half thousand years ago whilst the Babylonian empire was at its zenith.

How marvellous and beyond understanding are the providences of the Almighty. Ponder for a moment. Had the Lord not used the Babylonians to route and punish his rebellious Jewish people, Daniel would never have found himself in Babylon. Had he never gone to Babylon, he would never have stood before the king. The Spirit of God would never have made him ready to reveal the meaning and import of the vision. The result would have left believers, in the God of Israel and His Messiah, deprived of this wonderful prophetic outline of the ages. Here, contained in this portion of the divine record, we are presented with indisputable proof. God exists. He sees all of history from its beginnings to its consummation (Isa. 46:9-10).

Daniel stood before the king and boldly began. *"You, o h king, are the head of gold"* (Dan. 2:37-38). Babylon, that great empire was the head of the image. The prophet continued. After the Babylonian empire, other empires would follow. Each of these empires would, themselves, be succeeded by another until the coming of the Messiah would destroy the fifth. Has any of this come to pass? Yes it has. Three successive empires followed Babylon, making four in total so far. The Medo/Persian, the Grecian and the Roman Empires followed after Babylon. These four great world empires each rose, conquered the known world and then fell into the trashcan of history.

For years the legends surrounding ancient Babylon were thought to be just that? Legends and nothing more. According to ancient sources, the city of Babylon was one of the wonders of the ancient world. Built across the Euphrates, the river, their water supply, actually ran under the walls, which covered an incredible one hundred and ninety six square miles. It would take you three days to walk from one side of the city to the other. This was indeed the New York of the ancient world. The moat, surrounding the outer walls, was thirty feet wide. The outer walls were eighty seven feet thick. It was said the Babylonians could drive six chariots abreast along the top. The height of the walls was said to have been three hundred and eleven feet with two hundred and fifty watchtowers a further one hundred feet higher.

The outer wall also possessed one hundred gates, which were huge and made of solid brass. Once inside this wall, one was met with another smaller defensive wall before actually entering the city itself. Small wonder, then, on opening chapter five of Daniel we read how, in later years, king Belshazzar, of Babylon, successor to Nebuchadnezzar, was in the process of throwing a party, whilst outside, an invading army, led by Cyrus the Persian, was seeking ways to take the great city. To all intents and purposes, Babylon was impregnable, unconquerable. But the God of Israel, the God of Daniel, had other plans. And his plans, no high walls, no great army, no force on the face of the planet, can deny. This heathen monarch, in throwing this party, had not only challenged the enemy at his gates but had defied and insulted the Holy One of Israel. For as he and his friends and concubines ate and drank themselves into a drunken orgy they did so using the golden vessels taken from the very Temple of God in Jerusalem. Vessels dedicated as "Holy unto the Lord". May I ask you, how does that relate to you and I? As believers we are vessels of God taken from the dirt of sin, just as gold is taken from the fallen earth. We are touched by a Holy God, forgiven, cleansed, made new and clean and pure as gold. As such we are to be totally dedicated to the Master's use are we not? The hands of the world are not to touch us. We are not to go back to the dirt from which we were hewn. What an indescribable honour it is to be a Christian and to be chosen by God himself to be his vessel, taking the living water of the good news about Jesus the Messiah to a thirsty world, yet all the while not being part of the world system. Not bowing down to their gods of money, drugs, unlawful sex, power, an entertainment industry singing the praises of this world's values and so on. We too must come out from among them. We are to be different. With different values, different goals that honour God and not His fallen creation. Oh for a heart totally His! God help us to leave the false glitter of this doomed world system behind us. Turn your eyes to the home prepared for you in Heaven where your true citizenship resides. Use the resources, inventions of the planet that will aid you to serve the Lord. But keep away from all that would taint you, all that would seek to defile you and your testimony before God and men. Be a dedicated vessel!

As the king and his partygoers were feasting and drinking, the orgy came to an abrupt end as a disembodied hand appeared before them. They became quivering wrecks. The king literally shook in his boots (Dan. 5:5-9). The hand sent from God wrote on the wall before the terrified group. *"MENE MENE TEKEL UPHARSIN"* (5:25). None could translate the mystical writing (5:8,15). Again God had His man at hand. A true man of God, not a man claiming to be what he is not. But a man with the very Spirit of the living God within him. Daniel, now very aged, was brought hurriedly before the terrified group who had by this time probably become totally sober (5:13). After being courageous enough to tell the king exactly where he had failed in life (5:17-25), Daniel gave the assembled group the terrifying interpretation of the message from the Almighty.

"God has numbered thy kingdom and finished it. Thou art weighed in the balances and found wanting. Thy kingdom is divided and given to the Medes and the Persians"(5:25-28).

Belshazzar at once ordered that Daniel should be robed in scarlet, with a gold chain about his neck and be known as the third ruler in the kingdom (5:29). The king, it would seem, tried to assuage the judgement of Daniel's God by honouring Daniel himself. But Daniel was merely the instrument of God.

Many years ago a great man of God lay dying. Friends from all over came to pay him their last respects. One such friend said to him "Now you go to your reward, dear friend. Just think how many men and women you have blessed in this life. How many you have led to the Lord. The great written works you leave behind will bless many generations to come and they will praise you and your memory. Is that not wonderful?" The aged saint smiled and said "I am simply the pen that has been used of God to write but for a short space of time. And now He lays me down. Should the pen be praised for writing? No! No! Give Him the praise." May we ever have such an attitude to our own ministries. We are but His instruments. He may use us when He wishes and lay us down when He pleases.

The king of Babylon made the same mistake many people make. He looked to honour the pen and not the writer. He sought to change God's mind by honouring Daniel. A tragic error. What would have happened, I wonder, if the king and his people had wept and repented before Daniel's God instead of trying to praise Daniel himself? I think the book of the prophet Jonah provides us with the possible outcome. But the king did not turn to the God of Israel in repentance. History and scripture record the result of an unrepentant heart. Daniel states in verse 30 of chapter 5, *"That night was Belshazzar the king of the Chaldeans slain."*

One wonders, was it the very hand and finger of God Himself that had spelled out the end of Belshazzar's empire? Was this the very same hand that had, centuries before, written the commandments in stone before His servant Moses on Mount Sinai? That hand once wrote in gracious, loving, tenderness, laws, guidance, for the spiritual and physical well being of God's people. Tonight that same finger wrote uncompromising judgement upon the degenerate king and his evil empire. Two Babylonians had defected that very night. Under cover of darkness they were taken to the tent of Cyrus, where they explained, to Cyrus and his generals, that if the river could be diverted, the army could march under the walls of Babylon, along the dried river bed, and into the centre of the city itself. And that is what happened. The great river Euphrates was diverted and the Persian army took the city, killing king Belshazzar. From that moment on, the empire of Babylon was over and the city began to lose its greatness and importance among the people of the east.

Over the centuries the city gradually deteriorated. Businesses and people began to move away. General Alexander the Great attempted to rebuild the city and its temples. He actually died there. But Babylon, that once great queen of the ancient world, was doomed. She gradually sank beneath the desert sands. She became a myth. A story of mystery, told around camp fires, of a city swallowed by the ever shifting sands of the desert. Told and retold until no one believed there had ever been such a great, living, vibrant, mighty, city as ancient Babylon. That is, until German archaeologists journeyed to the Middle East. In the course of their excavations they discovered Babylon. In some areas the ruins lay as much as thirty metres beneath the swirling sands.

The Bible was right. The scholars were wrong. There had, after all, been a great city named Babylon. And as the Babylonian empire was washed away into the world of myths and legends, the Medo-Persian empire, ruled by Cyrus and his vassal Darius the Mede, arose on the still warm grave of the Babylonian empire. Yet it too followed the path of its predecessor.

After the Medes and the Persians there arose the Grecian empire led by the brilliant tactician, Alexander the Great. Alexander spread his empire so far abroad that it is said he wept like a petulant child when he realised there were no more kingdoms to conquer. Yet he died and his empire was divided between his four generals. Following hard on the heels of the Greeks, history tells us the Roman Empire rose up, strong, mighty, crushing all who stood in her way. Yet in the fifth century Rome herself disintegrated into legend.

As we look with incredulity at the accuracy of Bible prophecy embodied in this vision we see history written in advance. Gazing at the statue portrayed in the dream of Nebuchadnezzar, we come finally, to the feet of iron and clay. The fifth empire. The final empire before the coming in power of the Messiah. But one may ask, "Did the Messiah not already come in the days of the old Roman Empire?" "Was not Jesus of Nazareth the Messiah?" Yes indeed he was and is the promised one. But first he came to die for man's sin. Soon, when the final Roman Empire has risen and rules the earth, he will return in flaming power to judge the sin of unrepentant men. It is a fearful thing to fall into the hands of the living God.

TODAY WE ARE WITNESSING THE BIRTH OF THE FIFTH EMPIRE BEFORE THE REIGN OF JESUS CHRIST

REVIVED ROME

Students of prophecy have long recognised the fact that the iron of Rome is still seen at the end. Yet in weakened form. She is mixed with clay. The revived empire would be seen as attempting to come together and forming a definite shape but for some reason not really adhering to one nations within this revived Roman Empire are constantly differing over one thing or another. But at the same time they are united in their quest toward the main goal. A united Europe. A united world. In our day we have reached the feet and ten toes of the image. One the proofs of the Bible being the word of God, is the evidence of fulfilled prophecy. No other religious writing can compare with the sheer audacity of the Bible which dares to foretell the future and, by doing so, places its whole credibility on the line. If its predictions fail in one point then it is not worth trusting, because so much more within its pages could be false. But if it is true, then, arguably, it is without doubt the most incredible book on the face of the globe. That fact alone would mean this book had its origin, not on earth, not in the mind of man, but beyond earth, beyond the solar system, beyond the very universe itself. It had to have originated in the heart and mind of God Himself! Its predictions have so far proved 100 % accurate. You and I have the privilege of holding within our hands the only true, authentic message from the Creator of the universe and beyond. And found within its hallowed pages we discover God's plan for planet earth. This book is a message from the Great and Mighty Lord God Himself.

Yet how many of us who call ourselves Christians barely open its sacred pages? We would sooner sit down in our homes and watch our favourite soap opera on television. Filled with sexual immorality and Godless world views. Never mind if it's Bible study night.

You can record the soap opera and watch it when you get in. We love to watch sinners' sin. We would never do it ourselves. But we don't mind watching the dirty deed being acted out in our living room! Is that the right lifestyle of people who believe they have been bought by the precious blood of Jesus Christ? People who hold within their hands the words of God himself?

To sit night after night and watch the world entertain itself with its sin which God hates? Is this the lifestyle of a people called by God? A people who will one day give an account of their stewardship here on earth? A people who hold within their grasp the very words of eternal life? Believe me today's professing Christians are in grave danger of taking on the world's values and ideas simply because instead of daily feeding on the bread of life, the Bible, they have allowed themselves to be fed a daily visual diet of sex, drugs, violence, bad language, loose morals, risqué jokes and a news media that is tainted by the world's values. All presented to them in the comfort of their lounge!!

Many discerning people believe we are being "dumbed down". Fed garbage through the media to keep us happy and uninformed while the powers that be prepare us for the coming World Government and World Religion. Worse still, many Christians are becoming so spiritually dulled in their thinking, they are being hoodwinked into accepting false teaching from the front of their own Churches. Teaching that just a few years ago would never have been accepted. This is paving the way for the coming great deception and the false One World Church into which many scripturally ignorant, spiritually underfed and weak "Christians" will be herded like sheep to the slaughter.

Today as at no other time since the first appearing of the Lord Jesus, we are witnessing Bible prophecy coming to pass almost daily. Fulfilled prophecy, which points to the near return of Jesus Christ to rule the planet. Yet sadly so many believers are blissfully unaware of the incredible period of time through which they are passing. Bible prophecies uttered thousands of years ago, all due to be fulfilled at around the same period of time, are coming true before our eyes. We live in stupendous days but much of the Church, let alone the world, is unaware of the momentous days that are suddenly all around us. The last days are, without doubt, upon us.

- We see national Israel reborn as predicted for the end times (Jer. 31; Amos 9; etc.)

- We see them gaining Jerusalem as predicted for the end times. (Luke 21:24)

- We see an increase of earthquakes, wars, famines and diseases as predicted for the end times. (Luke 21:10,11)

- We see the Roman Empire beginning to rear its head once again as predicted for the end times. (Dan. 2; Rev. 13 etc.)

These and many, many other events are screaming at us "Christ is returning!"
(For further information regarding these events please order " Signs of the End of the Age." on DVD: address at back of this book)

Now is the time to awake. Do not be spiritually asleep as many were when Jesus appeared the first time and they failed to regard the signs. This time when He appears it will be in fiery judgement as He descends from the Heavens to His beloved Jerusalem. Are you ready to face Him? This is not pie in the sky nonsense. It is truth supported by ancient predictions being fulfilled to the letter in these very days. May I plead with my readers to get back to the Bible. Let us recommit ourselves to the Lord. Understand the times and stand ready for the coming days. The time is short. Get ready.

Chapter 2

THE DREAM OF REVIVED ROME

In Daniel chapter seven the prophet himself is given a vision which corresponds to the empires we have looked at.

7:1 In the first year of Belshazzar king of Babylon Daniel had a dream and visions of his head upon his bed: then he wrote the dream, and told the sum of the matters.

7:2 Daniel spake and said, I saw in my vision by night, and, behold, the four winds of the Heaven strove upon the great sea.

7:3 And four great beasts came up from the sea, diverse one from another.

7:4 The first was like a lion, and had eagle's wings: I beheld till the wings thereof were plucked, and it was lifted up from the earth, and made stand upon the feet as a man, and a man's heart was given to it.

7:5 And behold another beast, a second, like to a bear, and it raised up itself on one side, and it had three ribs in the mouth of it between the teeth of it: and they said thus unto it, Arise, devour much flesh.

7:6 After this I beheld, and lo another, like a leopard, which had upon the back of it four wings of a fowl; the beast had also four heads; and dominion was given to it.

7:7 After this I saw in the night visions, and behold a fourth beast, dreadful and terrible, and strong exceedingly; and it had great iron teeth: it devoured and brake in pieces, and stamped the residue with the feet of it: and it was diverse from all the beasts that were before it; and it had ten horns.

7:8 I considered the horns, and, behold, there came up among them another little horn, before whom there were three of the first horns plucked up by the roots: and, behold, in this horn were eyes like the eyes of man, and a mouth speaking great things.

The ten horns on the fourth beast in Daniel's vision and the feet and ten toes of the image in Nebuchadnezzar's dream correspond to the fifth empire. The toes and horns represent 10 kingdoms or regions that will exist during the period when Antichrist appears. Horns in biblical Prophecy represent either particular people or centres of power. The little horn that rises from within the ten horns is the coming ruler of the Revived Roman Empire, the Antichrist, because this horn is given a mouth to speak. I repeat, today we are witnessing the birth of the Revived Roman Empire foreseen by the ancient king of Babylon and the Hebrew prophet Daniel.

We are at the feet and toes of the image of Daniel 2 and we have also reached the emergence of the final beast of Daniel 7. The two are related.

The ancient Senators, and the Caesars of Rome, believed a united Europe would help bring to an end wars and disputes between different ethnic groups. It has ever been the desire, since the fall of Rome in 476 A.D. to return all of Europe to one central European government and one leader. It has been the desire of kings, emperors, dictators and the Popes of Rome.

As the Roman Empire went into a death spin, the Roman Church, already powerful and influential within the empire, began to raise its head and carry on where the Caesars of Rome left off. The Pope even inherited the title once worn by the ancient Caesars, Pontifex Maximus. As successor to the Caesars, the Popes began to rule as powerfully, as any Roman emperor, if not more so.

Since losing much temporal and spiritual power in the Reformation of the 16th century and suffering even further loss in the 19th century, Rome has longed for and sought for ways to return to her former glory and power which she inherited from the Roman Empire. And she has actively made plans to fulfil that dream. The dream of a United Roman Catholic Europe has been kept alive for centuries. A simple study will show how the Vatican, in the hope of becoming the religion of Europe, has always been at the side of those wishing to return to the days of Roman style, anti-democratic, dominion.

In St. Peters, Rome, on Christmas day 800 a.d. when most of Europe was under the rule of Charlemagne the Great, the Pope anointed him and crowned him "emperor of the Romans." Charlemagne was the first emperor of non-Roman origins and the first German emperor of the middle ages.

In 962 A.D. Otto the Great of Germany began what became known as the "Holy Roman Empire" following his coronation in Rome.

In 1262 the noble German family of Habsburg took over the leadership of the "Holy Roman Empire."

Later in 1806, fearful that Napoleon I of France was about to take to himself the title of emperor, the last of the Habsburg emperors, Francis II, dissolved the empire over which his family had reigned supreme for centuries. Despite this move, however, Napoleon did declare himself emperor. He firmly believed Europe should be joined together in what he termed "The

United States of Europe." As Pope Pius VII stepped forward to crown the new emperor, Napoleon snatched the crown from the hands of the startled Pontiff. Placing the crown upon his own head, Napoleon said "I am a Roman emperor in the best line of the Caesars." But as history records, his dream fell into disarray when he was defeated at Waterloo in 1815 by the British army led by Wellington.

Years later however, the dream of a re-united Europe based on the model of the old Roman Empire was rekindled in 1870 by the German Count von Bismarck who announced the birth of the second Reich or "empire." He regarded the "empire" set up by Otto the Great as the first Reich. Wilhelm 1st of Germany was appointed emperor of the Reich and given the title "Kaiser" which is German for Caesar. Thus the dream of a Revived Roman Empire was still alive and well, in the heart of late 19th early 20th century Europe. There is much evidence to support the belief that the Vatican backed any nation, or dictator, desiring to re-unite Europe. Though the relationship between the Catholic Church and the European nations has sometimes been very volatile, exploding, on occasions, into open war between the supporters of each side. This conflict of Church and state will reach its ultimate fulfilment when the future "ten kingdoms" of the Antichrist turn on the Babylonian Whore (false Church) and destroy her (Rev.17:16,17).

In 1930 Sir Winston Churchill published an article in an American magazine entitled "The United States of Europe." Mirroring the ideas of the ancient Roman senate, the Caesars, Charlemagne, the Habsburgs and

Napoleon, Churchill expressed the desire that all Western Europe should band together, in order to put an end to war, in a "United States of Europe." He later made a further impassioned plea for Europe to unite when he spoke in Zurich in 1946. In many ways this speech was part of the catalyst for the founding of the Common Market, later to become the European Economic Community, which in turn evolved still later into the European Union.

However, in 1930, as Churchill wrote his article for American readers, two men were working fervently toward fulfilling, by force if necessary, their own agenda for the European nations. Mussolini in Italy and Hitler in Germany. Mussolini and his Fascists said it was Rome's destiny to be the centre of Western Europe. Meanwhile, Adolph Hitler had dreams of uniting Europe under the 3rd Reich (empire). Hitler identified the continuity of the "Holy Roman Empire" with the First Reich (962-1806), the Second Reich (1870-1918) and his own Reich, which he believed would last for 1,000 years. In actuality Hitler's empire lasted far less than its predecessors, 1934 to 1945.

We shall look at the Vatican involvement with Hitler. Hitler was a Catholic, as was Mussolini. Neither of these monsters has been excommunicated from the Catholic Church for their despicable deeds. The reason for this becomes clearer when one realises that Hitler's and Mussolini's dream for uniting Europe was, in many ways the same dream as that of the Vatican. The Vatican's plan has always been a united Europe. A Catholic Europe with the Pope as supreme spiritual, if not political head. Pope John Paul II may fail through age, but his successor will be hoping for the dream to become a reality in his reign.

Chapter 3

THE VATICAN, POLITICS AND WAR

It comes as a great surprise to many when they discover the Roman Catholic Church is not simply a religious entity, but it also has political ambitions. The Pope is not merely the spiritual leader of the Roman Catholic Church. He is also the head of a very carefully structured and politically motivated organism.

In the early years of the Roman Church, she ruled supreme. When the Pope spoke it was law. Having taken over virtually as the Roman Empire crumbled (in 610 A.D. emperor Phocas actually declared Pope Boniface IV to be an emperor) the statements and decrees issuing from the Papal throne outweighed the decrees of emperors and kings alike. Rulers lived in fear of displeasing the Pope. To do so meant risking excommunication from Mother Church and being consigned to Hell. Many Popes were formidable military leaders who would send armies to subdue any nation or ruler daring to question the supremacy of the Church. Such rebellion would immediately invite the fiery wrath of Rome upon ones head. The Lord Jesus said *"My kingdom is not of this world"* (John 18:36). Apparently, the Pope of Rome believes otherwise.

Whenever a new Pope is enthroned, as the crown is placed upon his head these words are spoken: "(You are) Father of princes and kings. Ruler of the world. Vicar on earth of our Lord Jesus Christ". Also, the

Pope is crowned with a helmet shaped covering used originally by the deified kings of Persia (Babylon). This last fact, we shall discover, is highly relevant to our present study.

During the reign of Pope Alexander III (1159-1181), Frederick I, king of Germany, Italy and Holy Roman emperor, was excommunicated by the Pope. Frederick was furious and gathered his army, as did the Pontiff. In the ensuing battle, Frederick's army was soundly defeated.

In penitence and humiliation, the defeated emperor travelled to Venice to beg the forgiveness of Alexander III. After making the emperor wait outside in the snow for 3 days, the Pope emerged from his palace to receive Frederick's grovelling apology. When they met, Frederick removed his imperial mantel and knelt with his face and chest to the ground as the victorious Pope stepped forward and placed his foot on the emperor's neck (1).

Today the power of the Vatican is nothing like it was in past ages. Kings no longer tremble at the pronouncements of the Pontiff. But many Vatican insiders believe the Pope should have the authority to rule the world in the place of Christ. Over the centuries the Vatican and particularly the Jesuits have been working quietly, stealthily, to regain Rome's lost authority in the hope of establishing the Roman Catholic Church at the centre of European and world affairs. Those who believe the Vatican has no growing political or religious influence today should seriously study the facts of recent history and present day events in Europe and elsewhere around the globe.

The cover blurb to the insightful biography of Pope John Paul II, "His Holiness", calls him "the man who changed our century." "the foremost political figure of our time"(2). In it the authors reveal that in the 1980's the Vatican and especially John Paul II had a special relationship with the then director of the C.I.A. William Casey and the Reagan administration. Casey, a devout Roman Catholic whose home was "full of statues of the Virgin Mary" (3), visited the Vatican at least 6 times supplying the new Pontiff with political information from around the world to which very few were privy.

This very day Vatican Ambassadors (nuncio's) sit in residence in the capital cities of the world. And the world sends Ambassadors to Vatican City. What other religion has Ambassadors? Rome has because she is far more than simply a religious institution. She has enormous political ambition and influence. Evidently, Vatican Ambassadors take precedence over all other Ambassadors. These men are incredibly influential when speaking to the world's political heads of State. Rome boasts a following of 1 billion people. Therefore, when the representative of 1 billion people speaks in your ear, you listen. Make no mistake about it; the Vatican plan is to return to the influence and power she once held in Europe before the Reformation.

We shall be looking at Rome's actions in the past when before and after the Reformation she attempted to overthrow biblical Christianity with the use of force and bloodshed. Today she is using a silk glove, and soothing words to woo her "separated brethren" back into the fold. But any form of unity must be on Rome's terms and Rome's terms alone. The plan is to bring all of Europe, including Great Britain, back under the yoke of Rome. Predominantly Protestant England is known in Catholic circles as "Mary's dowry." Without a doubt the plan is make the religion of Rome the religion of every man woman and child from the Atlantic to the Urals and beyond. This plan includes Great Britain and the United States.

Historical events within Europe, when closely scrutinised, will at some point, usually reveal the hand of the Vatican. From the time of the Caesars onward men have looked forward to reviving Rome. Since the fall of the Roman Empire and the subsequent emergence of the Roman Catholic Church, the Vatican has longed for, and made plans for, a revived empire with herself at the head. The present E.U. is her vehicle to achieve that end. Included in the Vatican plan for a revived empire, of course, is the plan for all Europe and beyond to be united under one religion. The Roman Catholic religion.

In 1588, the Spanish Armada set sail, to bring Protestant England back under the dominion of the Pope of Rome. As they sailed they carried with them the Pope's promise of complete forgiveness to the man who could assassinate the Protestant Queen Elizabeth I. God saved England with the intervention of Sir Francis Drake's fleet of warships, plus severe storms which left much of the Spanish fleet at the bottom of the English Channel and at various other locations as far north as Scotland.

Less than half the ships that set sail managed to limp back into the safety of Spanish ports.

In the 19th century, under the blessing of the Vatican, Napoleon attempted to invade England and bring her under his (French) Roman Empire. Just as William the Conqueror had, with the Papal blessing, brought England under the heel of Rome after the battle of Hastings in 1066. Being unable to invade England, Napoleon turned his attention to Russia and suffered terrible defeat.

Likewise, Hitler also attempted to make Great Britain a part of the empire of the Third Reich. His plan to invade England was named "Operation Sea Lion." Faced with certain defeat king George VI called the British people to a day of prayer. Britain was hopelessly outnumbered and ill prepared to meet the German war machine. Manufacturers hurriedly churned out the needed weaponry. In the air the German Luftwaffe reigned supreme. Yet after that day of prayer and the subsequent Battle of Britain, the air force, outnumbered 3 to 1, somehow managed by the sacrifice of her young pilots, some barely out of school, to defeat the might of the hitherto undefeated Luftwaffe. One wonders how we would fare today were such a threat upon our doorstep.

As a direct result of God's answer to the nation's prayers Hitler, imitating Napoleon, turned his wrath toward Russia and God rescued England from the threat of the Nazi jackboot. And, of course, with the entry of the United States into the war in 1942, Hitler was eventually defeated. In all, king George VI called the British nation to prayer 5 times during the Second World War and God answered every time.

Since 1066 and William the Conqueror's Norman invasion of England, all attempts to conquer the British people have failed by the providence of God. Yet what these would be emperors, dictators and vassals of Rome could not do, we in these closing days of history have foolishly achieved in their stead. We have given away our own freedom, our right to govern ourselves. We, in Great Britain, are now at the mercy of the rising Roman Empire. And whom do we see, behind the scenes, quietly preparing to mount and steer this beast of an empire? The Roman Catholic Church.

The First and Second World Wars, when closely viewed, reveal the involvement of the Vatican.

Before the outbreak of the First World War, it was plain to see what was coming. Serbia, comprised of Orthodox Christians was looked upon by Roman Catholicism as " ..a consuming disease"(4). A threat to Russia and the newly birthed Roman Catholic state of Croatia. And, some supposed, a thorn in the side of the Roman Catholic, Habsburg family. Serbia must be crushed.

The Vatican Secretary of State, speaking explicitly on behalf of Pope Pius X, stated in 1914, shortly before the outbreak of the war "(The Pope) deplores the fact that Austria ha(s) not before this, inflicted upon the Serbs the punishment they deserve"(5). This and other statements issuing from the Vatican seem to have encouraged an attack upon Orthodox Serbia. This was part of the catalyst, the spark, which ignited all Europe into a war costing millions of lives and resulting in the re-shaping of the European nations.

The Vatican plan was then, and is now, to rid Europe of the memory of the Protestant Reformation, as well as Orthodox believers, and return the populace to Roman Catholic hegemony. The Austria-Germany coalition was defeated in 1918 and the Reich (empire) under Kaiser Wilhelm vanished. But at that precise time, a little Austrian corporal named Adolph Hitler began a transformation that would shake the world. In years to come he would become leader of Germany and the Third Reich, friend of the Vatican and author of the untold suffering of millions upon millions of human beings. The reason for their suffering? To fulfil his dream of a pure Aryan race. He would "cleanse" Europe of "lesser beings" and unite it under the Reich (empire). But what, you may ask, was the name Hitler gave to his dream of a united Europe?

The "European Economic Community"!

But in those days the prophetic time was not right. You live in the time that is right. God's time.
This is time of end time prophetic fulfilment.

In 1919, an overweight Italian ex-schoolteacher and journalist was on the rise to infamy and power. His name was Benito Mussolini, founder of the Italian Fascist Party. Although Roman Catholic, Mussolini was in reality, an atheist. As a young man he had dared God to strike him dead. When this did not happen he concluded there was no God. The Vatican eventually signed a concordat with Mussolini in 1929. The Pope said this atheistic Fascist leader was a man "sent by providence" (6). The reason for the Pope's support of Mussolini was easy to see. The Vatican had lost considerable temporal power. First in the Reformation, and later during the 19th century when in 1860 Italian Nationalists had annexed almost all the Italian states, once owned by the Vatican, apart from the lands immediately adjacent to Rome itself. They then handed them on a plate to the kingdom of Italy. As a result the Church's power, control and prestige within Italy suffered incredible damage both spiritually and financially. The 1929 concordat with Mussolini's Fascist state went a long way toward healing the wound. Prior to 1860, the Papal States covered almost sixteen thousand square miles within the borders of Italy. French soldiers protected the Pope until the fall of the French Empire in the late 19th century. The Italians seized Rome and Pius IX beat a hasty retreat into the Vatican, where he and his successors remained virtual prisoners until 1929, with the signing of the Mussolini concordat, known as the Lateran Treaty. The Papacy did not regain its former secular power under this treaty. However, the Vatican State was created and political sovereignty was granted within Vatican City, with the understanding that **the Vatican would not become involved in politics**. To compensate for the lands the Vatican had lost she was awarded the modern equivalent of 85 million dollars (7). But the signing of the concordat ensured the Catholic Popular Party and the Catholic Church would be unable to oust the Fascists from Italy. The Lateran Treaty was signed in the Lateran Palace, Rome, by Cardinal Gasparri for Pius XI and by Italy's Prime Minister and leader of the

Italian Fascists Benito Mussolini who signed on behalf of king Victor Emmanuel III of Italy. One of the lawyers involved in the negotiations was the brother of Cardinal Pacelli, destined to become Pope Pius XII.

We shall now look at more recent history. The Second World War, which in reality was simply a continuation of the first. The quest to dominate Europe. We must delve into some distasteful facts in order to show the Vatican involvement with Fascism, Hitler and his plan for European domination.

The rise of Hitler and his plan to unify Europe simply fell into line with the Vatican's ancient desire for a Revived Roman Empire. As Hitler and the Nazi party became more powerful, the Vatican ordered the German Catholic political party, the Zentrum, to disband. The Zentrum was the only party capable of withstanding and possibly defeating the Nazi party. Whatever the reason for the Vatican order, it helped pave the way for the Nazis to tighten their grip on power. The Vatican then signed a short lived concordat with the Nazi regime for what Hitler called "a privileged position."

Involved in the signing was Cardinal Pacelli (seated centre) who by this time was Papal Nuncio to Berlin. On this occasion he was the signatory on behalf of the Holy See. Also visible, standing, to the far right is a little known Prelate, Montini the future Pope Paul VI.

From this moment on the Catholic hierarchy were seen at Nazi functions. Hitler seen here with Archbishop Cesare Orsenigo Nuncio to Berlin.

Hitler greeting Reich Bishop Muller and Abbot Schachleiter, September 1934.

In both Belgium and France "Catholic Action" movements were formed with the intention of promoting Catholicism. However, in both countries, involvement with supporters of Hitler and Mussolini was actively encouraged. In Belgium the Fascist sympathiser Le'on Degrelle worked hand in hand with Catholic Action led by Mgr. Picard and Canon Cardijin. The outward goal was to inspire Catholic youth.
The inward goal was to destroy democracy.

Le'on Degrelle saluting Nazi troops in Brussels

Following the death of Pius XI, Pacelli was elected Pope on March 2, 1939, his sixty-third birthday. His new title was Pope Pius XII. Three days after his crowning, Great Britain and France asked the Vatican to join with them in protest against the German annexation of Bohemia and Moravia. The Pope refused. The Vatican stated it had no interest in politics. This simply encouraged Hitler to accelerate German preparations for war.

When Pius XII delivered his 1939 Easter message. He made a brief mention of broken peace treaties but failed to mention Germany. In fact, the new Pope sent a warm letter to "The Illustrious Herr Adolph Hitler.."

The Archbishop of Canterbury promised support if Pius XII would lead a new crusade against the Nazi aggressors. The answer was a firm, "No."

When Germany invaded Poland in September 1939, the Pope expressed his sympathy to the Polish people, but made no mention whatsoever of German aggression. After all, in 1929 the Vatican had agreed not to get involved in politics.

When war did break out on the third of September 1939, the Jesuits, whom we have already stated were created to counteract the Reformation, said "Germany's war is a battle for Christianity." (8)

In France the aged Marshal Petain became the puppet leader of "Vichy" after the German invasion.

It is interesting, to say the least, when one reads what the French newspaper "La Croix" (the cross) had to say regarding the close relationship between the policies of Petain and the ideals expressed by the Vatican.

In the early days of the war, the Vatican sent a plea to Great Britain begging the government to make peace with Hitler.

Following the assassination attempt upon Hitler in November 1939, the Pope sent him a personal note of congratulations on his "miraculous" survival.

Many ordinary Catholic lay people, priests and nuns, Protestants and those of no faith at all did risk their lives rescuing and hiding Jews and others during the war. When the war ended, as the allies entered Berlin, 1,100 Jews emerged from the safety of their hiding places where heroic Germans had kept them hidden throughout the war, right under the nose of the Nazis. During the war many Catholics and others stood up to the Nazi monsters and were made to suffer for their heroism.

Certainly, many of the German Catholic Bishops were deeply upset over the apparent silence of Pius XII, when he could have spoken out against the deportation and systematic extermination of European Jews. The Vatican received regular reports from all over Europe regarding the plight of the Jews and other minorities. Rome must have been aware of the unfolding human tragedy.

Today some believe Pope Pius XII remained silent because in 1942 an outcry from Dutch pulpits, in a letter of denunciation from the Catholic Archbishop of Utrecht, had resulted in the arrest of many Jews who had converted to the Catholic Church. Only time and God himself will finally reveal the truth of the matter.

The fact remains, the Vatican did virtually nothing to prevent the death of two thirds of European Jewry in the most appalling and heart rending horror of modern times. The Holocaust, known to Jews as "Ha Shoah."

When Germany attacked the Soviet Union, the German Bishops wanted to mount a crusade against communism. It would seem the Vatican considered it better to side with the Nazi regime than the "Godless" Russian Bolsheviks. After all Hitler was a Catholic and saw to it that Catholic schools and clergy were, in the main, unharmed throughout the war. Although some Catholic clergy and lay people continued to make a stand against the Nazi reign of terror and suffered as a consequence, it would seem the Vatican had its sights on the future and a few sacrifices here and there were apparently acceptable. After all if Hitler won the war he could unite Europe under the Roman Catholic religion and the Nazis.

In 1942, the Allies furiously denounced the extermination of European Jewry. They begged the Pope to issue a similar statement. The Vatican replied it could only condemn immoral acts in general. However, among the first Jews to be transported to Auschwitz were those transported from Slovakia. Wasn't that an immoral act? But the Vatican remained silent.

The head of the Slovakian Government was Dr. Joseph Tiso, a Catholic priest (9). We leave the reader to draw his own conclusions regarding the silence of the Vatican.

When Himmler, visited Rome in October 1942, he

"praised the 'discretion' of the Vatican." In 1943, the Nazis began gathering Rome's eight thousand Jews. The arrests began on October 15th. During the first round up over one thousand Jews, two thirds of whom were women and children, were transported to Auschwitz. As author John Cornwall writes in his book "Hitler's Pope" published by Viking Books, the trucks carrying them to their death actually passed St. Peter's Square and the residence of the Pontiff. The occupying German high command in Rome were concerned there may be an outcry from the Vatican to rally support for the Jews. To their amazement Pius XII remained silent. Even leading Nazis in Rome tried to privately circumvent the deportations for fear of a Communist uprising to rescue the Italian Jews. Many Italian Jews did manage to escape the Nazis. Sympathetic and heroic Catholics and others hid more than four thousand Jews in monasteries in Rome and elsewhere. It is also worth noting, not one Roman Catholic cleric was sent to offer succour to the inmates of any camp. Many would argue the wealth of the Vatican is due, in part, to Hitler and the Third Reich. Right up to the end of the war Germany continued to pay huge sums of money regularly into the Vatican coffers and some suspect the money flowed both ways. Hitler had met with the future Pope Pius XII as far back as the 1920's when the latter was Papal Nuncio to Berlin. During at least one meeting at Pacelli's residence the future head of the Catholic Church was seen to hand Hitler a large amount of "Church money" for his cause (10).

In 1942 Japan attacked Pearl Harbour, bringing the U.S.A. into the conflict. Within weeks the Vatican signed a peace pact with the Japanese government.

However, nowhere were the Vatican's true feelings toward democracy and Orthodox Christian believers in Europe more openly displayed than in Yugoslavia.

Here, in the early 1940's when it appeared Hitler's war was all but won the Catholic Church felt it was now safe to reveal its true heart and its dreams for Europe.

In Catholic Croatia, the "Ustashi", Croatian Nazi's butchered over 600,000 Serbian Christians in their fanatical efforts to produce a pure Catholic state.

Croatian Ustashi marching with Catholic nuns.

Leader of Catholic Croatia, Pavelic, decorating nuns for their Ustashi deeds

Anti Pavelic, leader of Catholic Croatia and head of

the Croatian version of the Nazis, the Ustashi, once stated: "He who could not cut away a child from its mother's womb is not a good Ustashi"(11). Pavelic kept several kilograms of his victim's eyes, as well as their gold and jewels. The incredible fact is we are writing of a man who enjoyed the favour of Rome. One who had audiences with the Pope. A dedicated son of the Roman Catholic Church.

While Ante Pavelic was turning Croatia into a pro-Nazi state, his right hand man, Archbishop Stepinac, organised the Catholic Church, encouraging a purge against Orthodox Serbian believers. The result was a Christian holocaust. Carried out on a smaller scale than the Jewish holocaust but every bit as deadly and terrifying for the victims.

Ante Pavelic's right hand man Archbishop Stepanic (front row right) seated with the Papal Legate Marcone, surrounded by Nazi and Ustashi officers.

The Ustashi were brutal in the extreme. Many of the officers were Catholic priests who donned the Ustashi uniform in order to carry out despicable inhuman atrocities against Orthodox Christians who had refused to change their faith to that of Rome. After becoming members of the Ustashi, some priests rose to become commandants of concentration camps.

Franciscan monk, Father Filipovic in his clerical dress and in his Ustashi uniform

One of the worst camps was Jasenovac where, for a time, Franciscan monk Father Filipovic became the commandant. The treatment meted out to the Serbian inmates was so horrific the camp equalled much of the horrors of Nazi death camps such as Dachau or Treblinka. More than 200,000 men, women and children were killed there. The camp was known as "Hell on Earth." As many as 40,000 innocents died in Jasenovac during Filipovic's administration. Father Filipovic daily visited the camp where he would cut the throats of Serbian women and children. He would also attack prisoners with a hatchet.

He became known as 'Father Satan'.

The Pit of Death
By kind permission: Alperin v. Vatican Bank
www. Vaticanbankclaims.com

One favourite mode of punishment, meted out to Serbian believers and others who refused to convert to Catholicism, was to send them to the "pit of death." Nothing too ingenious. Simply a huge pit where poor souls were buried alive for not becoming Catholic. The camp guards would hold competitions to find the "best throat cutter." An innocent prisoner would be dragged out of the ranks. His head would be held back while the guard would slit the pathetic souls throat for nothing more than sport (12).

Once whilst addressing a battalion of Ustashi in the village of Drakulic, Filipovic is said to have killed an Orthodox Christian child with his bare hands in front of them.

Many people in the camp were burned alive in brick

kilns. As one witness observed: "The cremation at Jasenovac took place in the spring of 1942... There was then a decision to *cremate people alive*, and simply open the huge iron door and push them alive into the fire already alight there. That plan, however, excited terrible reaction among those who were to be burned. People shrieked, shouted and defended themselves. To avoid such scenes, it was resolved first to kill them and then to burn them" (13).

Jasenovac Concentration Camp distinguished itself because of the number of young inmates sent there. In 1942 the Camp held over 24,000 Orthodox youngsters alone. Twelve thousand of them were said to have been murdered in cold blood by one of the camp Commandants. Prisoners who were sick or too old to change their religion were made to perish through neglect or were simply massacred. Christian Serbs as well as Jewish and Roma children were not spared, and special concentration camps were set up for them. Nine of these were at Lobor; Jablanac, near Jasenovac; Mlaka; Brocice; IJstici; Stara Gradiska; Sisak; Jastrebarsko; and Ciornja Rijeka. The destruction of infants in these places would be incredible, were it not vouched for by eyewitnesses, one of whom has testified: "At that time fresh women and children came daily to the Camp at Stara Gradiska. About fourteen days later, Vrban [Catholic Commandant of the Camp] ordered all children to be separated from their mothers and put in one room. Ten of us were told to carry them there in blankets. The children crawled about the room, and one child put an arm and leg through the doorway, so that the door could not be closed. Vrban shouted: 'Push it!'

When I did not do that, he banged the door and crushed the child's leg. Then he took the child by its whole leg, and banged it on the wall till it was dead. After that we continued carrying the children in. When the room was full, Vrban brought poison gas and killed them all" (14).

At his trial after the war Ante Vrban, who was said to be a pious Catholic, protested indignantly when he was accused of having killed hundreds of children.
He asked the Judge to consider the accusation a lie, "Since," he explained, he had killed personally
"only sixty-three of them." More than 240,000 Serbian believers were forced to convert to the Catholic Church. On December 21st 1941, the village of Mosanica was surrounded by the Ustashi. A monk from the Capucine Monastery told the terrified people: "You Serbs are condemned to death, and you can only escape that sentence by accepting Catholicism."

Forcible conversions became the standard practice of Ustashi Croatia. New converts were granted immunity from arrest, loss of property and from execution. Father Srecko Peric, of the Gorcia Monastery told the Ustashi: "Kill all the Serbs. And when you finish come here, to Church, and I will confess you and free you from sin." This call resulted in the deaths of 5,600 Serbs in one day, August 10th 1941.

After the war much of the gold taken from victims was found in Catholic Church vaults and even beneath a monastery altar. Remember the Vatican was apparently against Serbia because the Orthodox Serbian Christian beliefs threatened to disrupt Roman Catholic control of the area. The Vatican held regular meetings with the leaders of Catholic Craotia's Ustashi regime as well as receiving regular reports from its priests.

One could go on relating the atrocities committed by the Ustashi and the Catholic clergy against the Orthodox Serbians and others. It is so well documented. It was a horror almost beyond belief. Babies, mothers and fathers hung alive on butcher's hooks for fun. Fathers watching their sons being hacked to death by hatchets. Mothers forced to watch as their sons had their throats cut before they, themselves, were defiled and butchered. Aged Orthodox priests beaten to death, burned, drowned or beheaded. The entire property of the Orthodox Church was confiscated. The Patriarchal Palace was taken over and put at the disposal of the Catholic Church. And for what? To create a Catholic Croatia and Catholic Yugoslavia. Many believe the Vatican knew full well what was going on. Despite claims that she was not informed, it was a well known fact that the Vatican was regularly kept up to date by her priests scattered throughout Europe. The Ambassador of France to the Vatican wrote in 1940 "The evidence of German cruelties is so abundant that Pius XII no longer feels entitled to doubt it."(15) This must have included those atrocities being committed in Yugoslavia. Yet not one word was heard in defence of the innocents that were being butchered daily in the name of Rome. This silence was for the most part echoed throughout Europe and Russia.

Ante Pavelic, centre, in April 1942 when barbarities were at their height, pictured with Croatian Roman Catholic clergy.

In France, Jewish children as young as 2 years old were transported to death camps where they were exterminated along with their nurses or parents who had accompanied them. On one occasion when the crematoria in Auschwitz broke down the children were thrown alive on to open fires. Yet, it was said the Vichy government of France took no decision in matters of deportation without the knowledge of the Roman Curia.

In Russia as German troops poured toward Leningrad, the Vatican was keen to be at the helm in the "conversion" of Russia. In 1941 Hitler "authorised Catholic missionaries to go to the new Eastern territories."

As we shall see later, the Catholic Church's drive

toward Russia was in response to a "message" from the Virgin Mary when she allegedly appeared in 1917 and requested that Russia be converted to her "immaculate heart." Hitler wanted domination. The Vatican wanted to fulfil the wishes of Mary.

The two partners moved eastward hand in hand on a sea of Russian blood. But Russia proved too strong for Mary and Hitler combined. The Nazis suffered their worst defeat as thousands of soldiers met their deaths amid the bleak, bitter winds and snow of the Russian winter. The same fate had befallen the troops of another Catholic dictator almost a century and a half earlier. Napoleon Bonaparte lost thousands of his troops in the Russian snows after failing to attack England and turning his eyes eastward. The old dictum still stands. "If history teaches us anything, it teaches we learn nothing from history." These two friends of the Vatican, Napoleon and Hitler, eventually met ignominious deaths. But the Vatican continued to dream of glory under the next aspiring European dictator. Whoever he may be.

The evil of Russian Communism was not defeated then. That day would have to wait for almost fifty years until the arrival of John Paul II. A Pope totally dedicated to Mary. Dedicated to seeing her wishes for a Catholic Russia turned into reality and Communist Russia relegated to history.

CHAPTER 4

THE VATICAN RAT LINES AND THE NUREMBERG TRIALS

With the end of the war, Hitler dead by suicide, and still un-condemned by the Church for his crimes, the Vatican made moves to aid Nazi, Ustashi and other war criminals, in their bid to escape justice. It is suspected by many that the Ustashi regime and the Vatican helped organise escape routes for war criminals out of Europe to Latin America. After all, they may be of use in the future to defeat communism and thus establish a Catholic Russia and a Catholic Europe. Many believe much of the wealth stolen from murdered Serbs, Christians, Jews and Roma people found its way to the Vatican. It is argued by many that it was later used to fund escape routes to South America for the guilty butchers, after they had been given refuge inside the Vatican and its precincts disguised as monks.

What was the Vatican post-war reaction to Archbishop Stepanic? Pavelic's right hand man and the instigator of so much suffering meted out upon Serbian believers. The man of whom the Vatican said "His Apostolate shines with the purest brightness." After serving time under house arrest for war crimes he was made a Cardinal. Today Pope John Paul II has taken the initial steps toward beatifying Stepanic. In his defence we must note that Stepanic initially supported the Ustashi but was reported to have later stood against the regime of terror he had helped bring into being.

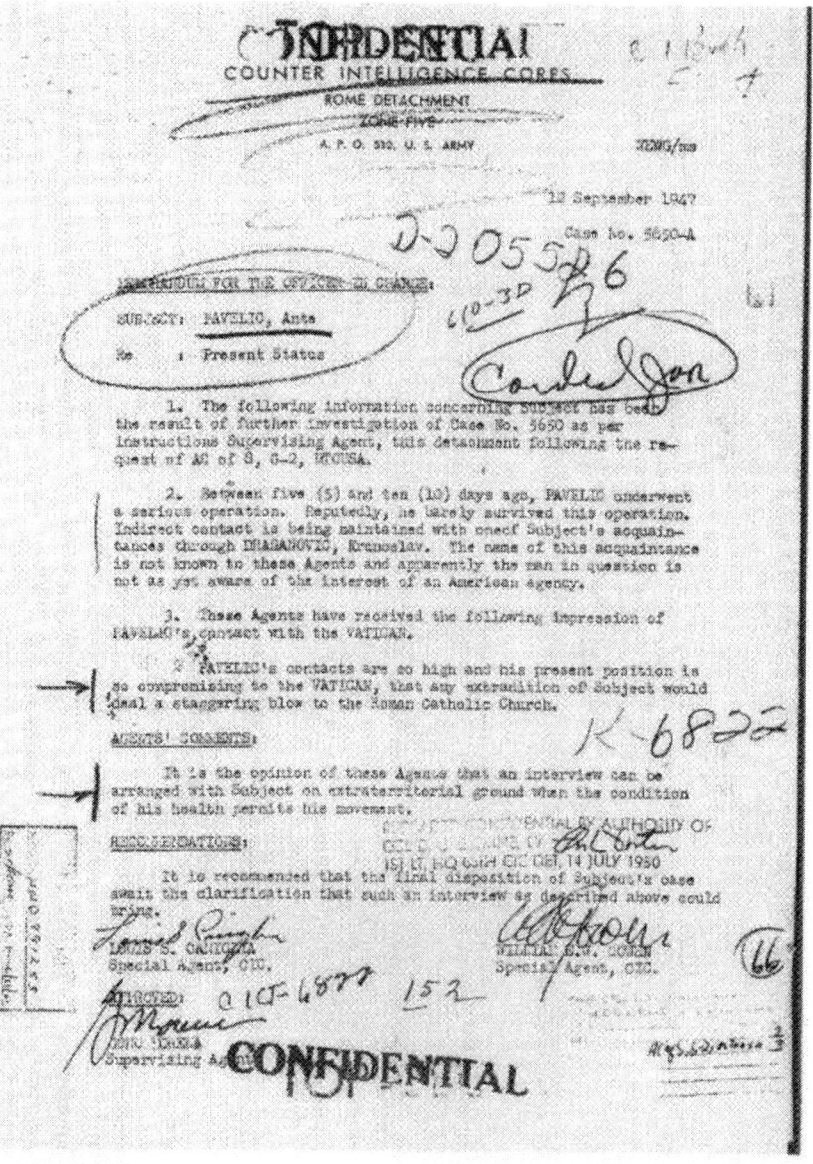

By kind permission: Alperin V. Vatican Bank. www.Vaticanbankclaims.com

When Ante Pavelic was finally discovered in Spain, the occupation security forces wrote a memo stating to have him extradited "would deal a staggering blow to the Roman Catholic Church." (point 4 over)

He finally made his way to South America where he lived in luxury until he returned to Spain in the 1950's. When Pavelic died in Spain in 1959, he received a special blessing from Pope John XXIII on his deathbed. This for a man whose regime had killed a third of the Jews, Serbs and Roma people of Yugoslavia, deported a third to the concentration camps, and forcibly converted a third to Roman Catholicism.

The Simon Wiesenthal Centre in Paris, an organisation which specialises in tracking down Nazi war criminals, has claimed the Vatican set up 22 committees after the War to help war criminals to escape. The murderers of thousands of innocents were issued with passports, and directed through a network of monasteries across Europe as they waited the opportunity to go abroad.

Adolph Eichmann, who engineered the operation to exterminate European Jewry, escaped through the Vatican "rat lines", eventually reaching Argentina where he lived in safety for the next 15 years. In 1960, the Israeli secret service, Mossad, and the Simon Wiesenthal organisation discovered his lair. Eichmann was drugged, kidnapped and hurriedly smuggled onto a plane. One can only imagine his sheer terror when this officer of the Reich, who organised the mass deportation of European Jews to certain death, awoke to find himself surrounded by the very people he had thought to exterminate. Not this only, but he discovered he was on his way to the Jewish state of Israel to stand trial before the survivors of the Shoah. In 1962 Adolph Eichmann was found guilty, hanged, cremated and his ashes were scattered.

People wiped his name from their minds saying "Eichmann is finished." But they are wrong. Adolph Eichmann's worst day is still future. One day he and his accomplices must stand before the Jewish Messiah Jesus and the God of Israel, to be sentenced for all eternity.

The Vatican is said to have also provided a means of funnelling stolen Nazi gold bullion into safe banks beyond the reach of the Allies. A US Treasury document based on intelligence information, accused the Vatican of keeping tons of Holocaust gold on behalf of the Fascist Croatian Ustashi. The Vatican said that the claims were untrue.

Today legal action is being desperately resisted by the Vatican as Serbian and Jewish survivors of the Nazi and Ustashi regimes seek an accounting for stolen World War II assets in a San Francisco Federal court (16). The Vatican dogmatically refuses to open its files in order to quash accusations that it colluded with the Nazis during World War II. In recent days the Simon Wiesenthal Centre approached the Pope and voiced their concerns about the matter. Pope John Paul II did not even acknowledge their request. They proceeded to approach the Secretary-General of the Vatican Committee on Relations with Judaism, Mgr Rémy

Hoechman, but he too refused to open the all important files. Even the U.S. Secretary of State Madeleine Albright twice asked John Paul II to open the Vatican files but was rebuffed. Also, the Vatican has recently been accused of being the main destination of over $55 billion in illegal Italian money alone. Many observers believe the Vatican Bank's hierarchy are hiding behind the benign image of Pope John Paul II. A recent report in one of Britain's leading newspapers named the Vatican as a top "cut out" country for laundering money. A "cut out" country is one whose banking secrecy makes it all but impossible to trace laundered funds back to their source. Files in the Vatican Bank are not retained after 10 years.

At the Nuremberg trials, in 1946, Hitler's willing murderers were tried for their hellish crimes against humanity. Daily they were faced with chilling and heart breaking testimonies from the mouths of survivors. Yet amazingly in the face of the horrific evidence, the voice of the Vatican was heard repeatedly pleading for the court to spare the lives of some of the Nazi monsters.

Oswald Pohl, the man who ordered concentration camps to be fitted with gas chambers, was sentenced to death. Pius XII sent him a message "Unjustly condemned by men, thou shalt find thy reward in Heaven. I assure thee" (17).

Another of Hitler's henchmen, Baron von Weiszaecker, made his escape and found sanctuary within the Vatican.

The Vatican reluctantly conceded to the Allies demands and handed him over for trial. Von Weiszaecker was sentenced to a mere 7 years imprisonment, for deporting French Jews to Auschwitz and actively preventing the Swiss Red Cross from saving French Jewish children. But a special plea for clemency had been read to the court. A plea from Pius XII (18). And this pleading for mercy upon the guilty was heard again and again from the Vatican What of Mgr. Tiso of Slovakia who sent Protestants to concentration camps and was responsible for sending the very first train load of Jews to Auschwitz? The allies executed him as a war criminal. The Vatican mourned him saying "He was a martyr."

In Yugoslavia the new government under Tito tried Father Filipovic, former commandant of Janesovac concentration camp, for war crimes. He was executed as a war criminal. Yet even on the gallows 'Father Satan' wore his Franciscan robes with pride. Today the Franciscans continue to deny any responsibility for the actions of Filipovic and other priests involved in genocide. But there is huge controversy as to whether the Franciscans ever condemned or censured Filipovic for his crimes. Many observers and investigators believe there was an enormous cover up that continues to this day.

In Italy, Mussolini and his mistress were denied the luxury of a trial. As they made a feverish attempt to escape the advancing allies, they were captured by Italian partisans who had them both shot. Their bodies were then subjected to repeated beatings.

They were finally strung up by their heels in the forecourt of a gas station in the centre of Milan. Even though Italians, in general, were relieved to see the demise of Mussolini it was said the Catholic Church held daily masses for the peaceful repose of the dead Fascist, and like Hitler, still Catholic, monster.

Did the Vatican remain silent during the war, as many claim? Paradoxically we read in the New York Times of March 14 1940 "Pope is emphatic about a just peace: Jews rights defended." The New York Times Christmas editorial of 1941 praised the Pope for "putting himself squarely against Hitlerism." In 1942 the Catholic "Tablet" of London stated that Goebbels had issued pamphlets in many languages condemning Pius XII as a "pro-Jewish Pope."

I must confess the Pope may have been aware of the many Jews who were rescued by being hidden in and around Rome in convents, monasteries and other places, but said nothing to the Fascists.

Yet the balance of opinion would seem to sway toward the possibility of the Pope playing both sides, especially when in the early 1940's he may have been made aware through his network of informants that the American President, Roosevelt, was seriously considering entering the war. Most commentators would appear to side with the opinion that, concerning the well being of certain ethnic and political groups within Europe the Vatican in the main remained silent throughout the war years. Did she remain silent as some have claimed, in order to prevent an even greater massacre?

One can barely believe that a word of protest from the head of the Catholic Church would have prompted the Nazi's to do worse than they were already doing. Or could it be, as many believe, the Vatican had expected to see a united (Roman Catholic) Europe under the Nazi regime? A Europe over which she would weld immense influence as she returned to the days of glory she had known before the Reformation?

Yet in 1945 with her dreams of a revived Rome and a united Europe under the rule of the Vatican quashed again, the Vatican silently waited and dreamed of the next opportune moment for glory. It would not be long in coming.

Chapter 5

BIRTH OF AN EMPIRE

As the monsters of Nuremberg eventually danced on the end of a hangman's rope or vanished behind bars, one may have thought the Vatican dream of a united Catholic Europe had perished with the end of the war. But it did not. Through pressure from Catholic politicians, encouraged by the Vatican, the dream was rekindled in the heart of post war Europe. Only now the plan would be achieved by stealth rather than by bloodshed.

Catholic politicians worked so hard to birth the revived empire that Pope John Paul II is in the process of canonising the founders of the present day European Union. An act unprecedented in the history of the Catholic Church. To turn politicians into saints. John Paul II has also stated in the European Parliament that the Catholic Church could be "instrumental in uniting Europe from the Atlantic to the Urals." This is virtually the same phrase used by Hitler when he described his desire for Europe. To unite Europe from the Atlantic to the Urals.

The dream lives on.

The Papal Ambassador (Nuncio) to Brussels has described the EU as "a (Roman) Catholic confederation of States." Rome's plan is to unite Europe politically and the world spiritually.

How will this be achieved? First by helping to birth a revived empire. Secondly by creating an ecumenical, all embracing, all accepting spiritual brotherhood. Based in Rome of course. But also in Jerusalem and possibly the ancient city of Babylon, Iraq. Also the Pope has said he would like to head the World Council of Churches from Jerusalem. Recently, he called Jerusalem "My second Vatican." Those who know their Bible will of course be aware the Antichrist and the false religious leader will have Jerusalem as one of their centres of operation. We will mention a little more on this point later.

Concerning Europe, the encyclicals of Pius XII and John XXIII stated Europe would become "the greatest (Roman) Catholic superstate the world has ever known," "the greatest single human force ever seen by man", bound together, no doubt, by religion. Pope Pius XII made mention of this dream way back in 1952 in his Christmas broadcast. He stated his dream was to see "a Christian order which alone is able to guarantee peace. To this goal the resources of the Church are now directed." Indeed they were.

This is the Vatican which, as we shall see, tortured, burned and butchered true believers through the centuries. The same Vatican that helped Hitler's rise to power. The Vatican whose Pope blessed Mussolini's troops and blessed his war planes as they prepared to bomb defenceless Abyssinia. The Vatican, which remained practically silent as Hitler's henchmen, murdered six million European Jews alongside countless numbers of others deemed unworthy to live in a pure Aryan world. It is the Vatican which supported the Croatian Ustashi as they slaughtered the Orthodox Serbian, Jewish and Roma population and forcibly converted many of the survivors to Roman Catholicism. The Vatican which operated almost unhindered throughout war torn Europe. In France at the side the Nazi, Vichy, puppet government. In Belgium, Holland, right across mainland Europe Rome moved freely among the Fascist rulers, saying nothing as millions perished under her nose. Yet this same Vatican was later heard pleading for the lives of Hitler's henchmen and actively aided others in their bid to escape justice. It is the Vatican whose motto is "always the same", meaning she has not changed one of her anti-scriptural beliefs or her dreams of power. Yes, it is the very same Vatican continuing to prod and push Europe from behind the scenes toward the realisation of her dream.

That dream is on our doorsteps even now.
Its name?

The E.U. or the Revived Holy Roman Empire.

From the very birth of the Common Market or the E.U. as it has become known, Rome has been involved.

In 1956, on the Capitoline hill in Rome, the first 6 signatories of the "treaty of Rome" signed the document founding the Common Market. The signatories were; Germany, France, Italy, Belgium, the Netherlands and Luxembourg. As they walked away to their respective diplomatic convoys, one later recalled "We all felt like Romans." On that historic day former

Belgian Prime Minister and one of the founding fathers of the present E.U. Paul-Henri Spaak, stood beside John Rockefeller and said "I believe we have revived the old Roman Empire without firing a shot."

As the "Common Market" was born scholars of ancient Bible prophecy sat upright realising that what they were witnessing could be the birth pangs of the prophesied revival of the Roman Empire. A prophetic fulfilment so full of implications. The pinnacle of which would be the arrival of the Antichrist and his ultimate defeat at the return in power of the Messiah, Jesus. It is most interesting to note: Germany and France have, for centuries, been at the forefront of European political integration. From Charlemagne to Napoleon, to Hitler on to the present day, it is France and especially Germany who have led the rest of Europe toward a revival of the Roman Empire.

The European Monetary System (E.M.S.) was brought about, in 1978, mainly by the initiatives of two men. The German Chancellor, Helmut Schmidt and French President, Vale'ry d'Estaing. Similarly, in 1990, the desire for monetary and political union, sprung from two men, Helmut Kohl, Germany's Chancellor, and Francois Mitterrand President of France. Chancellor Kohl has said: "The future will belong to the Germans ... when we build the house of Europe." Once again as in past European history, we witness Germany and France pushing for closer European unity. If we look closely we see the Vatican peering from behind the stage curtains, patiently manipulating the strings of the empire through its puppet adherents.

Bernard Connolly is former head of the European Commission responsible for analysing both the European Monetary System (E.M.S.) and National and Community money policies. In 1995 he wrote "The Rotten Heart of Europe" published by Faber and Faber. The book is a devastating exposé of the European plan for monetary union. Bernard Connolly believes the move toward monetary union is "part of a programme to subvert the independence - political as well as economic - of Europe's countries" (19). The oft stated phrase "The joining together of European nations is purely economic and not political" is a complete fallacy. At present 12 member nations of the E. U. have adopted the Euro and discontinued their old currencies some of which had been in use for centuries. On the eve of the monetary changeover, the President of the E.U. Romano Prodi was asked "… it is a political project isn't it?" He smiled and replied "This is not economic. This is a pure political process" (20). That is from the mouth of the President of the E.U. as he was interviewed on British television! The monetary union is not economic. It is a pure political process.

Also, Mr. Connolly believes there will eventually be a hard core of member nations within the E.U. "that together made up the empire of Charlemagne" (21).

So the dream of Charlemagne and the Vatican is still alive and well. In 1996 Mr. Connolly was dismissed from his position after stating among other things, what he believes to be the truth behind the plans for European integration. The ordinary man and woman in the street have been hoodwinked into believing the E.U. is just the simple joining together of trading partners. It is that and more. It is also the fulfilment of the dreams of men bent on removing the sovereignty of nations. In the place of sovereignty, they wish to oversee the birth of a central government ruling the nations of the E.U. and eventually beyond. But of course many leaders of the E.U. will never tell you and I their real plans for us. And it seems they will dismiss any who blow the whistle on them and their nefarious plans.

Adolph Hitler is reported to have once said "If you tell a lie long enough, loud enough and often enough people will believe it." "People are more likely to believe a big lie than a small one." Hitler lied about the Jews of Germany and Europe. He portrayed them as subhuman and devious. Despite the fact that they were influential in banking, the arts, science, philosophy, literature, medicine and so on, Hitler, against all common sense, convinced most Germans that the Jew was a less moral, less than human, creature. Today we have been told untruths concerning the supposed benefits of joining the European Union and most of us have swallowed the lie. Today we are told, repeatedly, further European integration will not affect our national sovereignty. And most Europeans believe it despite facts to the contrary being patently obvious. Britain has very little sovereignty now.

Almost 80% of laws passed in Britain are issued from within the E.U. Our home made laws are now virtually worthless. Should any one disagree with British law the British government can be hauled before the European Court of Human rights or the Court of Justice. If Britain is ruled to be wrong, her government must amend the law and cow tow to Europe. Fifteen judges in Luxembourg are now the supreme creators of British law. E.U. law supersedes that of British law: "Every national court must apply Community law in its entirety and must accordingly set aside any provision of national law which may conflict with it" (22).

Lord Denning (former Master of the Rolls) said: "European law ... is now like a tidal wave bringing down our sea-walls and flowing over the fields and houses to the dismay of us all" (23).

The Maastricht treaty of the early 1990's ensures that Brussels rules Britain in over 70 areas including: taxation, monetary policy, education, immigration, judicial policy, health and safety, industrial policy, energy and so on. Germany's foreign policy spokesman has said that Germany not only wants a federal Europe, but that member states sovereignty has already been lost, the idea of sovereignty is "an empty shell", he said. Yet the British people are for the most part unaware that their political and religious sovereignty is now almost totally a thing of the past.

Lord Tonypandy, retired speaker of the House of Commons and a Christian, wrote to The Times on 24/4/95: "The current slide towards a single European currency threatens both our economic and political independence, and thus our sovereignty. Subterfuge and half truths have been used to persuade the nation that neither our sovereignty nor our relationship with the Commonwealth is endangered." He said.

German MEP (Member of the European Parliament),

Otto von Habsburg, is an ardent Roman Catholic. He is also a descendant of the family that ruled the Holy Roman Empire from the 13th until the early 19th century. In 1989 he stated: "Europe is living largely by the heritage of the Holy Roman Empire." However, senior British Parliamentarian Hugh Gaitskell, foreseeing the true cost of joining the "Common Market" as it was then known, said of this rising empire way back in 1962, we have lived to see "the end of almost a thousand years of British history."

We are assured "This is not a Superstate." Then pray tell me what is? The E.U. now has a passport, a flag, an anthem, and since January 1st 2002 a common currency. That, to many, constitutes a Superstate. Soon we shall have our own army, emergency task force, possibly a Navy and an air force. What will follow....our own state religion...the Roman Catholic religion? Prophetically speaking, this is where we are today. We are watching the birth of a Revived Roman Empire as prophesied by Daniel (Dan.2, 7 etc) and the aged apostle John (Rev. 13, 17, 18).

The historic plan of the Vatican for a united Europe is on course. That which we are witnessing today in Europe is the embryonic fulfilment of Daniel's prophecy. The ten toes of the image are taking shape. This rising empire, many believe to be a fulfilment of ancient biblical prophecies. Godly men, who have studied the Bible over the centuries, firmly believed the fulfilment of Daniel's prophecy, and John's in the Revelation, would herald the return of the Lord Jesus Christ. Dear saints went on to their reward wondering just when the end would come and Bible prophecy would be vindicated. But here we stand, in the cold dawn of the 21st century. Citizens of the Roman Empire whether we want be or not. Yet witnesses to the veracity and trustworthiness of the prophetic word of God.

In the future this burgeoning empire must encompass most, if not all, the earth. We can only watch and see. Certainly, within the E.U. today, we are witnesses to the fact that this is the first time since the fall of the Roman Empire so many nations of Europe have banded together. The single currency is now in the hands of some member states. That is the first time since the days of the Roman Empire that Europe has had the same currency.

Soon, no one knows how long, the footsteps of the Antichrist will be heard echoing through the halls of this rising empire. Make no mistake about it he is coming and may be alive at this very moment. Breathing the same air, looking at the same sky, walking beneath the same sun as you and I.

And all the while waiting for his star to rise when he shall step out of the shadows and into the full glare of the worlds' adoring eyes. He will draw the nations together in a common cause. Possibly through some real or contrived threat to world stability and security. Eventually under this man's rule, believers in the uniqueness of the Christian faith and of Jesus Christ will be persecuted without mercy as will the Lord's own race the Jewish people. His persecution will make both the Inquisition and the Holocaust pale in comparison.

And the Church at large is ill prepared to warn of this impending tragedy. Why? Because they are asleep to the urgency of the hour. The leaders are telling their flocks "all is well" when all is not well at all. In fulfilment of ancient prophecies of a falling away from the truth, many are leading their Churches back to Rome. Back to a Rome that, as we shall presently see, continues to teach and encourage belief in pagan spirituality.

We in Britain are now at the mercy of the rising Roman Empire. An empire foreseen by the prophets of the Bible. An empire that will birth the greatest and most hideous dictator the world has known. The man the Bible calls Antichrist. At his side will be the false world Church led by the "false prophet."

At the end of the Second World War Paul-Henri Spaak said "We do not want another committee. We have enough already. What we want is a man of sufficient stature to hold the allegiance of all people and lift us out of the economic morass into which we are sinking. Send us such a man and be he God or the devil we will receive him."

One day Mr. Spaak's words will come true as the devil incarnate, the Antichrist, takes hold of the reins of this new empire we see, even now, rising before us.

How many today are even slightly aware of the momentous period through which they are passing? The period immediately preceding the arrival of the man of sin. The Antichrist, his empire and the birth of an all encompassing false world Church. Christians who are sounding the alarm are looked upon as being fanatics. Poor deluded folk who are so Heavenly minded they are no earthly good. The real truth is so many in the Church are bogged down with the cares of this world. Or else they have been taught a false triumphalism which says we (the Church) will take over the world and Christianise it. Only then will we invite Jesus Christ to return and take over the Earth! These poor sheep fed on false doctrine by false shepherds, do not see the true signs of the end when they are right before their eyes. The Lord Jesus Christ told the religious leaders of His day who failed to realise he was the predicted Messiah *"You know how to discern the face of the sky but you cannot discern the signs of the times"* (Matt. 16:3). So it is today. So many are able to understand many things in this modern world but are unable to discern the most important events. The predicted signs declaring the soon return of Jesus Christ. Many "believers" enjoy living in Egypt so to speak. They have their cars, their homes, and their holidays abroad. When someone tells them "these are the last days", they do not look with joy for the Lord's return.

Instead they fear his return will herald the end of their comfortable lifestyle. These believers have become so Earthly minded they are no Heavenly good. They block out the truth by giving the stock answer "He may not come for a thousand years. No one knows when he will come back." It sounds rather like the rebellious Israelites at the foot of Mount Sinai. "As for this Moses, the man that brought us up out of the land of Egypt, we wot not what is become of him" (Exodus 32:1). But Moses did return and so will the Lord Jesus Christ. But first will come the Antichrist. Friends, now is the time to awake for the signs of his arrival are becoming clearer by the day. Awake, awake for the night is almost upon us.

If we return to the dream of king Nebuchadnezzar, we are told that a stone cut without hands crushed the feet of the image and became a huge mountain which filled the earth (Daniel 2:34-35, 44-45). Hallelujah! That is a picture of the Lord Jesus returning to the earth, to the Middle East, destroying the fifth empire, the World Government of the Antichrist, and setting up his own kingdom on earth, in the Jewish city of Jerusalem.

Please do not think when we speak of these things we are meaning the end of all life on the planet. What we are looking for is the physical return of Jesus Christ to the planet and the setting up of his kingdom of peace.

That is surely something to look forward to if you are a Christian. If you are not then you should be getting worried because Jesus Christ is coming back to judge the rebellious inhabitants of planet earth. And that means you if you have never given your life to Jesus Christ. But read on and you will discover He not only loves you, though neither you or I deserve His love, but He has also provided a way for you to escape His righteous judgement.

In 1997 I stood on the Temple Mount in Jerusalem. I gazed eastward across the Kidron valley and up into the blue sky above the Mount of Olives. As I did so, I thought of the book of the prophet Zechariah, chapter 14:1-5;

1 Behold, the day of the LORD cometh, and thy spoil shall be divided in the midst of thee.

2 For I will gather all nations against Jerusalem to battle; and the city shall be taken, and the houses rifled, and the women ravished; and half of the city shall go forth into captivity, and the residue of the people shall not be cut off from the city.

3 Then shall the LORD go forth, and fight against those nations, as when he fought in the day of battle.

4 And his feet shall stand in that day upon the mount of Olives, which is before Jerusalem on the east, and the mount of Olives shall cleave in the midst thereof toward the east and toward the west, and there shall be a very great valley; and half of the mountain shall remove toward the north, and half of it toward the south.

5 And ye shall flee to the valley of the mountains; for the valley of the mountains shall reach unto Azal: yea, ye shall flee, like as ye fled from before
the earthquake in the days of Uzziah king of Judah: and the LORD my God shall come, and all the saints with thee.

Here, in this wonderful portion of the unerringly accurate word of God, we are told of a still future event. The day the Lord himself shall descend from the Heavens and his feet shall stand upon the Mount of Olives. From there he will defeat the assembled armies of the Antichrist. Also if you are a believer in the Lord Jesus, you will be there with the Lord on that day (verse 5). You do not have to be created a saint by the Pope of Rome. Every believer who trusts Jesus for his or her salvation is a saint in God's eyes. So says the Bible.

Believers in the New Testament were constantly addressed as "saints". So even if you have never been to Israel, one glorious day God will give you a trip, for free. One day. One fabulous day we shall be with him in the skies over Jerusalem, His beloved city. What a day to look forward to. All troubles over. No more tears, pain, suffering, broken dreams. No more sad partings. Just forever with Jesus in His kingdom. What a glorious future the followers of Jesus have in store. Lord hasten the day.

But to return to our present study. Concerning the ten toes on the image in Daniel chapter 2, do not Daniel 7 and also John writing hundreds of years later in the book of Revelation chapters 12, 13, 17 and 18 also give us a picture of ten horns? Revelation tells us the ten horns on the beast are ten kingdoms or rulers who receive rulership at the end of the age under Antichrist once the new empire has emerged.

12 And the ten horns which thou sawest are ten kings, which have received no kingdom as yet; but receive power as kings one hour with the beast. (Rev. 12:17)

The ten toes on the image signify the same as the ten horns of Daniel 7. Both visions represent the evil empire of Antichrist, which Jesus will destroy. But if these are the last days, where are the prophesied ten kingdoms over which Antichrist will rule? Are we able to see them today?

The Club of Rome is a very, very powerful political group indeed within Europe. Under the secretive plans of politicians, bankers, Freemasons, the Council on

Foreign Relations and numerous other bodies planning a World Government, the Club of Rome has been given the task of uniting Europe and dividing the world into manageable blocks. Just a short time ago, the Club of Rome submitted a plan to the United Nations, one of the main movers toward a One World Government. The plan was to divide the world into ten regions. By 1996 the United Nations had done exactly that.

THE WORLD DIVIDED INTO 10 REGIONS

AS SUGGESTED BY THE CLUB OF ROME AND ESTABLISHED BY THE UNITED NATIONS

Ten Kingdoms Set up by The Club of Rome.

(1) U.S.A.; CANADA; MEXICO
(2) WESTERN EUROPE
(3) JAPAN
(4) AUSTRALIA, NEW ZEALAND, SOUTH AFRICA
(5) EASTERN EUROPE INCLUDING FORMER U.S.S.R.
(6) SOUTH AMERICA
(7) NORTH AFRICA, MIDDLE EAST
(8) REST OF AFRICA
(9) SOUTH & SOUTH EAST ASIA
(10) CENTRAL ASIA

This division of the world is now commonly accepted and followed in the world of computing and banking. Notice how the affluent areas of the world are first.
(1) U.S.A. Canada   (2) Western Europe   (3) Japan.

The Bible says in Daniel 7:24 three of the ten are conquered or taken over by the beast, the Anti- Christ.

24. And the ten horns out of this kingdom are ten kings that shall arise: and another shall rise after them; and he shall be diverse from the first, and he shall subdue three kings.

Is that not interesting that the three areas at top of our list are the three that rule the world, so to speak. These could change as the days progress. Australia could become one of the three should America fall from her present lofty position. The Australian lifestyle has already overtaken that of the USA. If Anti- Christ were to gain control of these three "power blocks" he would indeed be the most powerful man on the planet! How could John the Apostle writing the book of Revelation on a little island in the Aegean sea 2,000 years ago, possibly have known that at the same time the Roman Empire was being re-formed the whole planet would be divided into ten regions. Totally astounding! Totally impossible unless God told him in advance.

As an aside in late May 2002 Switzerland became the last nation to join the United Nations. The U.N. and the E.U. are working in ever closer harmony and this author believes that one day in the not too distant future the two will merge and be based within the confines of the old Roman Empire. How this will come about I do not know but I believe the Bible is clear. Antichrist's kingdom must be based within the old Roman Empire.

Now the whole world is at the mercy of the rising government. The Vatican, although not a member of the U.N., is so involved in U.N. affairs that her membership is an unspoken reality. Her influence within the halls of the United Nations and the European Union is well known. Her influence is global.

The feet of Nebuchadnezzar's image represent the Revived Roman Empire, and we see it being birthed today. It will eventually govern the earth. Amazingly, in the year 2000 the heads of over 150 nations met in New York to discuss the possibility of World Government. This surely must mean the stage is being set for the coming of the Antichrist. What a truly incredible, yet pivotal, time to be alive.

Friends, if we see all these things coming to pass, we must ask "Where is the woman who sits upon the beast of the Revived Roman Empire in Revelation 17? Is she Rome? Is there any further evidence or clue to the identity of this mysterious woman?"

In our next chapter we shall endeavour to discover the identity of the woman who rides the beast.

Chapter 6

MYSTERY BABYLON THE GREAT, MOTHER OF HARLOTS AND ABOMINATIONS OF THE EARTH

Rev 17:1-18

1 And there came one of the seven angels which had the seven vials, and talked with me, saying unto me, Come hither; I will shew unto thee the judgment of the great whore that sitteth upon many waters:

2 With whom the kings of the earth have committed fornication, and the inhabitants of the earth have been made drunk with the wine of her fornication.

3 So he carried me away in the spirit into the wilderness: and I saw a woman sit upon a scarlet coloured beast, full of names of blasphemy, having seven heads and ten horns.

4 And the woman was arrayed in purple and scarlet colour, and decked with gold and precious stones and pearls, having a golden cup in her hand full of abominations and filthiness of her fornication:

5 And upon her forehead was a name written, MYSTERY, BABYLON THE GREAT, THE MOTHER OF HARLOTS AND ABOMINATIONS OF THE EARTH.

6 And I saw the woman drunken with the blood of the saints, and with the blood of the martyrs of Jesus: and when I saw her, I wondered with great admiration.

7 And the angel said unto me, Wherefore didst thou marvel? I will tell thee the mystery of the woman, and of the beast that carrieth her, which hath the seven heads and ten horns.

8 The beast that thou sawest was, and is not; and shall ascend out of the bottomless pit, and go into perdition: and they that dwell on the earth shall wonder, whose names were not written in the book of life from the foundation of the world, when they behold the beast that was, and is not, and yet is.

9 And here is the mind which hath wisdom. The seven heads are seven mountains, on which the woman sitteth.

10 And there are seven kings: five are fallen, and one is, and the other is not yet come; and when he cometh, he must continue a short space.

11 And the beast that was, and is not, even he is the eighth, and is of the seven, and goeth into perdition.

12 And the ten horns which thou sawest are ten kings, which have received no kingdom as yet; but receive power as kings one hour with the beast.

13 These have one mind, and shall give their power and strength unto the beast.

14 These shall make war with the Lamb, and the Lamb shall overcome them: for he is Lord of lords, and King of
kings: and they that are with him are called, and chosen, and faithful.

15 And he saith unto me, The waters which thou sawest, where the whore sitteth, are peoples, and multitudes, and nations, and tongues.

16 And the ten horns which thou sawest upon the beast, these shall hate the whore, and shall make her desolate and naked, and shall eat her flesh, and burn her with fire.

17 For God hath put in their hearts to fulfil his will, and to agree, and give their kingdom unto the beast, until the words of God shall be fulfilled.

18 And the woman which thou sawest is that great city, which reigneth over the kings of the earth.

In Revelation 17 we read of a woman sitting on the back of the beast of a Revived Roman Empire. The woman has a title on her forehead. Mystery Babylon the Great. Mother of harlots and abominations of the earth. When the apostle John saw her he was amazed for that is what the old word "admiration" means in verse 6. Up to this point we are not told of John being even slightly phased by any of the things he had seen. I am sure he was. But this time when he looked upon the woman and the beast, he wrote *"I was amazed."* He was stunned. He was shaken. Why?

As a harlot this woman is totally different to the bride of Christ, the Church. The bride of Christ is always pictured as being chaste, virginal, set apart. These two women could not be any further apart. They are total opposites. Throughout the Old Testament the Lord always likened Israel's apostasy, her going after foreign gods as spiritual harlotry. Spiritual adultery. Spiritual whoredom. It is the same here. The harlot John saw is a false Church. A false religious system, endowed with great influence and power in the last days. A religion claiming to basically follow Jesus, yet prostituting her faith with all and sundry.

The true Church of Jesus Christ unites with no one other than those who acknowledge Jesus as Lord and him only as our means of salvation. In my Church we sing, "on Christ the solid rock I stand. All other ground is sinking sand."

The true Church would never say "Jesus is one way. But your way will also get you to Heaven if you are sincere." The true Church would never say "Jesus' death saves you but you must also do this, as laid down by Church tradition, before you can get to Heaven." But these statements are made by the Roman Catholic Church to those of other faiths and to their own followers. Therefore it is no surprise to discover when John saw the woman in Revelation 17 he was shocked and stared in great wonder! Is this the Church? It cannot be! What has happened? John was stunned!

Some may ask "How do we know this woman is Rome and the Roman Catholic Church? And if we are able to prove that point, what role has the Vatican played in the spiritual history of Europe and what influence does she weld inside the present day European Union?" Also what are her plans for us?" All this will become clearer as we progress. First let us look at Revelation 17.

In verse 18 of chapter 17, we are told, *"the woman*

represents the city which rules over the kings of the earth." When the Apostle John wrote the book of Revelation, there was indeed one city ruling over the kings of the earth. That city was Rome. Indeed Christians living in the first centuries of the Christian era used the code word "Babylon" when speaking of pagan Rome.

In verse 15 we read she *"sits on many waters."* Whereas land or earth usually depicts Israel or the Jewish people in prophecy, waters represent the Gentile nations. Indeed the ancient Roman Empire ruled over very many people across the European continent, North Africa and the Middle East. Likewise today the Roman Catholic Church boasts a following of over 1 billion people across the globe!

Now to the very interesting verses 9 and 10. The 7 horns of the beast are hills on which the woman sits. Rome is known as the city of the seven hills. She was indeed, built on seven hills. Something that can be said of no other major city. So that is yet another clue concerning the identity of the city which will be the base of the coming false One World Religion.

Also we are told the 7 horns represent 7 kings or kingdoms. Five had already fallen when John received his vision. One was and one was yet to come. Indeed, the empires of Egypt, Assyria, Babylon, Persia and Greece including the total rule of their kings had all passed into history when John wrote the book of Revelation. One of the 7 was still in existence. Rome and its emperor. And one was to come, revived Rome and its leader. And out of the seventh empire will arise one who is of the seventh. That is, the empire will evolve from the revived empire of Europe into a world empire. Its sway will extend beyond the boundaries of the old Roman Empire and across the globe. The leader of this world empire may even be a former, present or future political leader within the nations of the present revived Roman Empire within Europe. He may even be a past, present or future leader of the United Nations which, as has been stated, is planning to bring in a World Government in the next few years. However I believe eventually the world will be governed mainly from within the old Roman Empire. How this will be achieved I cannot say. It is yet future. Perhaps some awful catastrophe will engulf the United States as God removes His hand of blessing from the USA and the balance of world power will shift to the European continent. Or perhaps some international emergency, threat or catastrophe, real or even contrived by the powers that be will draw the majority of the nations to rally around one banner under one leader. From this future empire will emerge a leader who will hold sway over the entire world. Again, his base will be within the old Roman Empire. But his rule will be over the earth.

Many people believe the Pope will be this leader. Indeed they believe the Pope *is* an Antichrist who will one day become *the* final Antichrist world leader. Personally I find it difficult to hold to this view because chapter 18 of Revelation says the 10 kingdoms will hate the false Church and destroy her. Yet Antichrist is clearly seen at the end of days leading his armies against various rebellious nations and finally against Israel and her returning Messiah (Dan. 11:35-45; Rev.19:19:20; Zech. 14:1-5). If the Pope of Rome is to be the Antichrist, could he survive if his world Church fell? Or indeed is he the False Prophet who will support the Antichrist? That of course presents all kinds of interesting avenues of discussion which we cannot go into now. Yet there are those who believe the Antichrist will be a Gentile because he rises out of the sea (Rev. 13: 1,2), synonymous in scripture with the Gentile nations.

Also, the False Prophet could be a Jew because he arises from the earth (Rev. 13:11), usually representing Israel or the Jewish people. Scripture is crystal clear that at the end when the true Messiah, Jesus, returns in power Israel will still be in existence. She will be in turmoil. In dread danger. Perhaps even on the very verge of total defeat. But she will be rescued from all her foes by the returning Jesus who will set up His glorious kingdom in the city of His Jewish ancestor, king David (Zech. 14). My speculation is that a future Pope of Rome could very Charismatic in personality and charismatic in his spirituality. This would give him great acceptance among many Protestant charismatics. And although the religious Jews will view him as a traitor to the faith of Judaism he may well win their undying affection by fulfilling their centuries old dream for the building of a new Temple in Jerusalem. A Temple which, after 1260 days of a Middle East peace, initiated or "confirmed" by this Roman leader, he will defile (Dan.9:27; 11:31; 2 Thes. 2:4). If future events come to pass in this way a future Pope could fit the frame for the False Prophet. He will lead many blind spiritual heads and their equally blind followers into a new age of spirituality. A new age where all men are equal and all beliefs, apart from the truth, are able to find their own niche in the New World Religion.

To reiterate, my own suspicion at this time is that the Antichrist will be a political figure who allows the false World Religion based in Rome to have sway for a while then when he no longer needs her he will destroy her. the False Prophet will very possibly be a Pope of Jewish origin who will hang onto power by being the right hand man of the Antichrist. I am sure my brothers in the Lord Jesus will have reasons for not following my train of thought. So be it. Let us not break fellowship over this point. We can agree the Pope of Rome is an Antichrist and a final Antichrist is to come. Just who he will be and who the False Prophet will be is all yet to be revealed.

If proved wrong I shall be the first to apologise to my brethren. In much of prophecy we see through a glass darkly. Bible prophecy is proven in retrospect. Looking back we see the fulfilling hand of the Almighty. Let us watch with baited breath as Bible prophecy unfolds and becomes clearer before our ever widening eyes. When it does come to pass we shall know it.

Whichever view of the coming leader is correct the clear word of God declares Antichrist will lead a world empire arising from the Revived Roman Empire we see being birthed before us in the E.U. today. Within the United Nations and the E.U. there are many political groups and organisations, some we named earlier, linking both sides of the Atlantic together, all seeking one goal. World Government. One of the most powerful and influential groups is the highly secretive Club of Rome which has, as has been noted, influenced the United Nations into dividing the world into ten regions.

Among other groups working toward a One World Government are:

U.N.
E.U.
THE ILLUMINATI
INTERNATIONAL FREEMASONRY
ROCKEFELLER FOUNDATION
ROYAL INSTITUTE FOR INTERNATIONAL AFFAIRS
BILDERBERG GROUP
TRILATERAL COMMISSION
COUNCIL ON FOREIGN RELATIONS
G7
WORLD BANK
THE PARLIAMENT OF WORLD RELIGIONS,
THE STATE OF THE WORLD FORUM
INTERNATIONAL MONETARY FUND
THE UNITED RELIGIONS

The above groups and others, are all working feverishly to sweep you and I into a new world where we are ruled by one central government with one all encompassing World Religion. Do you not see how, despite its authors being separated by hundreds and even thousands of years, the Bible hangs together. One scripture compliments and enhances another. Daniel compliments John and the Revelation even though they were separated by 500 years. The Revelation expands on Daniel, Zechariah and many other Hebrew prophets. Many of them separated by centuries. What an incredible book the Bible is.

Let us continue to look at Revelation 17. The woman

is dressed in purple and scarlet (Rev.17:4). The emperors of Rome would dress in these very colours. How interesting to find the Roman Catholic Church dresses her Popes, Cardinals and Bishops etc. in the same colours.

She is arrayed in gold and precious stones (Rev. 17:4). The wealth of the Vatican is said to be greater then the combined wealth of France, Germany and Great Britain. Her holdings run into Billions. Need we also mention the indecent wealth the Church spends in order to dress the images of the saints in golden cloaks or crowns encrusted with jewels while many of her adherents live in abject poverty.

Revelation 17:4 states that the cup the woman holds is full of abominations. All the people have been made drunk by her wine. She invites all to come and drink and in so doing share in her abominable acts. Rome has seduced many professing Christians and Politicians into committing spiritual adultery with her. She also makes overtures to, and woos, the followers of pagan religions into her bed alongside blind "Christians" who are blissfully unaware of the slippery path they are on.

What an abomination it must be in God's eyes to see those who profess to follow Him and His Son cavorting with those who deny and reject Him.

Also, although many Popes lived exemplary lives, many did not. For instance, Pope John XI (931-936) was the illegitimate son of a previous Pope, Sergius III (904-911).
The nephew of John XI was Pope John XII who was

eventually deposed following charges of adultery, perjury, murder, incest and sacrilege.

Pius II (1458-64) openly admitted he had fathered at least two illegitimate children by two different women, one of whom had been married at the time of their affair.

Pope Alexander VI (1492-1503) was a member of the infamous Borgia family and was also the father of six illegitimate children, two of whom were born after he became Pope. His daughter was the equally infamous Lucretia Borgia whose marriages were arranged by her father in order to extend his power and influence. When the reformer, Savonarola, attempted to have the Pope deposed, the Pope arrested him and had him condemned as a heretic, hanged and publicly burned.

One Pope said that to lay with a boy or a woman was no greater sin than rubbing one's hands together. Many Popes were open adulterers, fathering children from their numerous affairs. Many of those in the lower orders of the Church were no better. In the 12th century Cardinal John of Crema chided English clerics for their sexual liaisons with prostitutes. However, the same clerics surprised him that very same night by entering his room and discovering him with a local prostitute.

More than one Pope died at the hands of an angry mob or suffered death under the blows of a jealous husband. In fact so many Popes and clergy either fathered illegitimate children and placed them in high office or were illegitimate themselves Pius II stated

"Rome is the only city run by bastards." And yet we are asked to believe these men are the legitimate successors to the apostles of Christ. And the Church declares the Pope is not to be judged by any man (24) or court (25). Moreover since 1870 the Catholic Church has decreed the Pope to be infallible when making declarations concerning doctrine. This includes the declarations of all previous Popes regardless of behaviour. Yet how are we to accept such obvious heresy? Over the centuries many Church councils have condemned and dropped some overtly heretical and immoral Popes from the official Vatican list of Popes. But herein lies the problem for Rome:

If the Pope is infallible how can he be condemned and dismissed as a heretic for making declarations he believes to be true? To add to the nonsense of Papal infallibility many Popes openly disagreed with the former occupants of the Vatican.

Gregory I (590-604) said anyone who took to themselves the title "Universal Bishop" was an Antichrist.
But Boniface III (607) was given the title "Universal Bishop" by Emperor Phocus who also declared the Pope to be an emperor.
Pope Hadrian II (867-872) stated all civil marriages were lawful.
But Pope Pius VII (1800-1823) declared them illegal.
Pope Eugene IV (1431-1447) sentenced Joan of Arc to be burned as a witch.
In 1920 Pope Benedict XV declared her to be a saint.

Some Popes even had their predecessors exhumed

from the grave and put on trial for heresy! But we are told that in matters of doctrine they are infallible! The teaching of infallibility goes against the clear word of God not to mention common sense and the record of history. The doctrine of Papal infallibility is not a Christian doctrine. It is a further sign of the unchristian beliefs within the Vatican. Also at least two Popes have been suspected of being murdered by Vatican insiders because they had drawn up plans to change the corruption within the Church.

Included in the cup of abominations seen in Revelation 17 is Rome's twisting of, and adding to, the scriptures. For instance, in some Catholic books I have seen the Ten Commandments presented with the commandment against graven images removed. How is this achieved? By simply dividing the tenth commandment into two, Rome still comes out with ten. Also because the Church teaches "Mary is ever Virgin" when in Matthew 13:55-56 the neighbours of Jesus ask *"Is not this the carpenters son? Is not his mother called Mary? And his brothers James, Joses, Simon and Judas? And his sisters, are they not all with us?"* the Roman Catholic Church has in some cases weaved around this obvious denial of Mary's perpetual virginity by calling Jesus' brothers and sisters "cousins."

This playing with and adding to scripture is a precursor to drawing souls away from salvation, not toward it. As we shall soon see, Catholic souls are taken down a dark and infernal trail of laws and observances at the end of which is Hell itself. Surely, this alone is an abomination to God.

You see the picture below is of a woman holding a goblet. Notice, also, the crown she wears. The crown is similar to the type worn by the ancient Caesars, who, as high priests of Pagan Rome, wore a crown portraying the rays of the sun. Need we mention the similarity between the woman and the Statue of Liberty which stands on Ellis Island. New York.

Woman with cup from Rome, on reverse of medal. —(ELLIOTT'S Horæ.)

A point worth reflecting upon which investigative readers would find rewarding.

In verse 6 of Revelation 17 we are told the woman is *"drunken with the blood of the saints."* In the past this woman, Rome, has murdered the saints of God, (not to mention those of other faiths). She is pictured here drunk with their blood. Rome under the Caesars inflicted untold suffering upon the Christian Church of the first 3 centuries. Men, women and children were given over as sport for the masses. Nero had many crucified, covered with pitch and set on fire. Others had to endure the howling mob of the arena as they were eaten alive by lions, tigers and other creatures, deliberately half starved for the gruesome spectacle.

However, "Christian" Rome was equally eager to rid

the world of true believers in Christ. Any other group, ethnic or religious, who dared to disagree with the Vicar of Christ was also hounded, if possible, out of existence. It has been estimated that somewhere in the region of 60 million Christians alone have been martyred by the bloody hands of the Church of Rome.

Imagine the countless lives lost through her persistent persecutions through the centuries. The Inquisition, for instance, where Jews were forced to eat pork and confess to being a Christian on pain of death. These "chosen" people were herded from one city to another. From one country to another, from continent to continent and in many cases at the command of the Vicar of Christ sitting in Saint Peter's chair. And today the Vatican continues to side with Israel's enemies. When Pope John Paul II visited Israel in 2000, he travelled part of the time in an Israeli ambulance. However the Israeli's were ordered by the Vatican to remove the Star of David from the ambulance's side. Two priests with the same blood group as the Pope travelled with him. In case of an emergency the Pontiff would not have to call upon Jewish blood to save his life. Somehow the Pope seems to forget the Lord Jesus, who shed his blood on a Roman cross for him and all mankind was and continues to be Jewish.

Witness the long line of Christian martyrs who have suffered at the hands of Rome's emissaries and endured untold suffering before, during and after the Reformation and the Inquisition, so that we may have the freedom to read the Bible and proclaim the true Gospel. I have a very large book in my possession. It measures 11 inches by 8 inches and is almost 3 inches thick. Its title is the "Martyr's Mirror" (26). It chronicles the martyrdom of thousands of Christians who were burnt at the stake, countless bodies torn on the rack, beheadings, torn tongues, ears, hands, feet; eyes gouged, people buried alive, drowned, smothered, whipped, men, women and children who died in dirty, foul smelling, rat infested dungeons. Deprived of light, of food, of loved ones. Deprived of all but their faith in the word of God and in the Christ portrayed within its pages.

Who is responsible for these outrages? In most of these cases ecclesiastical Rome is responsible. Millions upon millions of Bible believers have been butchered in the name of Rome. Many believers suffered long before Luther nailed his 95 thesis to the door of the castle Church of Wittenberg at the beginning of the Reformation. These are facts of history about which many Christians are totally ignorant. Many are under the assumption that before the Reformation every one was a Roman Catholic. Not so. There were many who stood against Rome and her heresies. As a result of their brave stand, many paid with their lives in the most horrific ways invented by their tormentors. The Albigenses were one such company which preached against the corruption of the truth within the Catholic Church's teachings. In the 12th century they accounted for almost the entire population of southern France. By the end of the 13th century, thanks to a war of extermination waged by the Catholic Church, the Albigenses were wiped from the face of the earth (27).

In France on August 24th 1572, on orders from the

Vicar of Christ, more than 70,000 Huguenot's, were butchered in what has become known as the St. Bartholomew's day massacre (see above).

When news of the massacre reached Rome, Pope Gregory XIII was so overjoyed he went in grand procession to St. Peter's to give thanks.

The military director of this wholesale murder of innocent Christian men, women and children, regardless of age, was the Mar'echal Tavannes. As the slaughter continued he rode through the streets with his sword dripping blood, crying "Kill, Kill." Some years later as he lay dying in bed, he made confession of his sins to a Catholic priest. When the priest reminded him he had not mentioned the killing on St. Bartholomew's day he replied he regarded it as a "meritorious action, which ought to atone for all the sins of my life" (28).

In 1598 "The Edict of Nantes" was issued by King Henry IV of France, granting Protestants the freedom to live freely in French owned territory. This included freedom of worship, entry into French schools, Universities, and Colleges. The Huguenots were even permitted to build their own schools.

When news of the Edict reached Rome, Pope Clement VIII furiously summoned the French envoys to his presence. He stormed at them "…..I see an Edict the most accursed that can be imagined, whereby liberty of conscience is granted to everyone, which is the worst thing in the world" (29). This is a statement from one whom Catholics are expected to accept as a successor to St. Peter. A Pope who viewed "liberty of conscience" as "the worst thing in the world."

Almost 90 years later under Louis XIV, who had been reared by Jesuits who loathed the liberty given to Protestants, the persecutions began all over again. Christian men and women were hung from ceilings by their hair or feet in an effort to make them return to Rome. Some were bound, with funnels forced into their mouths. Wine would be poured down their throats until they were deprived of reason and enticed to sign a recantation. Others endured the untold agony of having molten lead poured down their throats and being left to die in utmost agony. Many were tied with long ropes and thrown into deep wells until they cried for mercy recanting their beliefs. Others were thrown into fires only to be dragged out and questioned as to whether they had decided to change to Catholicism. Failure to recant resulted in being thrown back into the flames. Further, even worse tortures, if one can imagine them, were carried out on defenceless believers in an effort to make them become Roman Catholic.

In 1685, October 17th, King Louis XIV signed the "Revocation of the Edict of Nantes." Every liberty formerly given to Protestants was revoked. Schools were closed. Places of worship were demolished. Protestant ministers who refused to leave France within 15 days or return to Roman Catholicism faced a life in the galleys. Protestant women who managed to escape torture were sent to convents for the rest of their lives. Ships leaving for England were ordered to be sprayed with poisonous fumes in order to gas any one attempting to stow away and escape. Many Protestants were simply murdered by the mobs. A deep spiritual darkness descended over France.

But Rome rejoiced.

When Pope Innocent XI was informed of the signing of the "Revocation" special prayers of thanks were offered and Rome was illuminated in celebration for 3 days. Innocent XI wrote to King Louis XIV "....The Catholic Church shall most assuredly record in her sacred annuls a work of such devotion to her and celebrate your name with never dying praises" (30). Bossuet, Bishop of Meaux, addressed the King in a

sermon "...You have confirmed the faith. You have exterminated the heretics" (31).

Yet thousands of Huguenots did manage to escape to England where their deep spirituality brought blessing to these Islands for many generations.

Many Catholic apologists argue that the Pope was not aware of the killings when he made the above statement. However it made no difference, for some time later when he would have been fully aware of all that had taken place, he had a medal struck in honour of the event.

Pius III is said to have had 60,000 people massacred in one day. An achievement he later viewed as the high point of his papacy (32). We mention France merely as an example. France was not the exception. This butchering of innocent believers who stood against the false teachings of Roman Catholicism was widespread. The Waldenses; the Hugenots; the followers of Wycliffe; the Lollards in England; the Albigenses; the followers of John Huss on the continent. One could go on recounting the bravery and sacrifice made by believers across Europe as they made their stand against the false teachings of Rome. These dear ones gave their lives for our spiritual freedom. A freedom many are bent on throwing away so easily today. These and millions of believers perished at the hands of Rome over the centuries in the most brutal of methods that could be devised.

In England Bishops Latimer and Ridley were just two out of thousands ordered to be burned at the stake for opposing Roman Catholic doctrine. Today these two great martyrs of the faith are largely forgotten. We should hang our heads in shame for ever forgetting the pains so many of our forebears went through in order for us to enjoy the freedom we have to preach the Gospel. We have forgotten the cost of our freedom.

One of the main differences in doctrine which led to so many believers being hung, burned, strangled and so on was centred around the question *"Does the bread of the Sacrament remain bread after the priest has prayed over it, or does it indeed become the very body, soul, Divinity of the Lord Jesus Christ?"*

Thousands of dear believers perished for simply affirming that the bread remains bread and God cannot be eaten. We shall look at this further in a moment. Suffice it to say for now, Charismatic preacher Benny Hinn stated quite clearly on American television, in front of millions, "When you eat this bread you are eating the body of Jesus." Seemingly Hinn and the Roman Catholic Church are in agreement in believing that the bread of the communion is the actual body of the Lord Jesus Christ, when scripture says plainly it is simply bread (1 Cor. 11:26,27) and is eaten in remembrance of Jesus' one and only sacrifice, not as a witness to its continuance on Catholic altars (Luke 22:19). In saying the bread is Christ's actual body Hinn has betrayed the memory of countless numbers who gladly died in order to preserve the belief that the bread is eaten simply as a memorial of Christ's death. Instead, Hinn regards counter doctrine and theology on the subject to be, "sick stuff." Or as Paul Crouch of Trinity Broadcasting calls it, "doctrinal doo doo." Basically the leader of one of the largest "Christian" networks in the world is saying certain doctrine is excrement. As we shall see, the Catholic Church believes every time a

Mass is held, Jesus is present. The bread having been transformed into His actual body, He is suffering on the altar every bit as much as He did on the cross.

In 1984 Arthur Blessit was interviewed by Paul Crouch on TBN. Blessitt described how he had received the Eucharist (Mass) while participating in a rally of 600,000 Roman Catholics in Poland. He said he first registered an objection when the priest came toward him for he knew that Catholic doctrine forbids giving the wafer to a Protestant. The priest said, "You're one of us," and Blessit accepted it. At that point the studio audience cheered and Crouch said, "The walls are coming down. His body is one. There's no difference." He went on to say that he was erasing the word `Protestant' from his vocabulary. "I'm not protesting anything," he said (33).

Also on his "Praise the Lord" show, Friday, May 31,1991, Paul Crouch announced that Benny Hinn was arranging a private meeting for him with Pope John Paul II. Crouch said that he would be asking "his Holiness" when the walls between Protestants and Catholics would come down and the Church would be one as Jesus asked the Father.

On his October 17, 1989 "Praise the Lord" show Crouch stated that "more than ten years ago" he had already declared that he was "eradicating the word Protestant from (his) vocabulary," that he was "not protesting anything anymore."

But let us return to our study of Revelation 17 and the woman drunken with the blood of the martyrs. The above facts must add weight to the identity of the woman in Revelation 17 being Rome and the Roman Catholic Church. While Protestantism can claim blood on its hands, Rome's are drenched with the blood of martyrs.

Yet what of the woman's name, Mystery, Babylon the Great?

According to ancient writers, the city of Babylon was founded by Nimrod, the grandson of Ham who, in turn, was the son of Noah. We read of Nimrod in Genesis 10. The writings of the ancient world agree with the biblical account. There was a man named Nimrod.

In Genesis 11 we read, as men travelled eastward after the flood of Noah, they came to a plain and built a city. Genesis 10:8-10 states that Noah's Great grandson, Nimrod built the city and named it Babel. Also, they began building a tower "that will reach up to Heaven." They built the city and tower in order to prevent themselves being scattered over the earth. The reason for the tower has been a subject of much debate. Many contend that the people intended to build a tower so high that should there be another flood they might escape by climbing unto Heaven. Both these acts would have been an act of defiance against God who had already stated in Genesis 9:1 "..fill the earth" and in 9:11 He had promised to never again cover the entire planet with a flood. Yet the people built a city to prevent being scattered and a tower in case God sent another flood upon the earth. So in order to fulfil His plans, and put and end to their rebellion God caused the people's speech to differ. In response to this judgement of God the people were scattered against their will, divided into different languages and eventually into different nations. Interestingly, recent research has revealed all languages have a single origin and the entire human race is descended from two original parents. The Bible has known this for thousands of years. The Bible tells us different languages originated from a single language at Babel and our first parents were named Adam and Eve. Christians need never feel challenged by science.

Science is daily proving the trustworthiness of the Bible.

As we study the history surrounding the different nations and languages emerging from Genesis 11 and the tower of Babel, we discover some very interesting points. It makes fascinating reading to discover what the ancients had to say about Nimrod. He had a wife named Semiramis. She was very beautiful but also very corrupt. We are told she was a very immoral woman. In various nations and cultures we find Nimrod and Semiramis deified. Central to the ancient worship of Semiramis and Nimrod was the death and supposed reincarnation of Nimrod.

When Nimrod died, Semiramis said he was the sun god. She later gave birth to a son, Tammuz. Semiramis proclaimed this child to be none other than Nimrod the sun god, reborn. As time passed, Semiramis herself was deified and proclaimed to be the "Queen of Heaven." As the sun god, Tammuz (Nimrod) and his mother Semiramis were believed to bring enlightenment to the world. In many ancient paintings they are depicted with a halo of light around their head. This has nothing at all to do with holiness. It is a picture representing the disc of the sun. A disc which was copied in edible form and eaten in honour of Tammuz the sun god and his mother the "Queen of Heaven."

In Jeremiah 7:7-18 the prophet condemned the people for making cakes to the Queen of Heaven (Semiramis). The cakes were actually circular, in the form of the disc of the sun in honour of her son the sun god. Today the Catholic Church continues this abomination. It holds processions in which the disc shaped wafer, the "Host" of the Mass is displayed in a sunburst. The Church believes the Host *is* the Lord Jesus Christ in edible form as was Tammuz. To those who know their Bible this is blasphemy.

The Bible clearly states that Jesus is in Heaven. That he suffered once for all men (Heb. 9) then ascended to Heaven (Acts 1). The Catholic Church however, teaches that Jesus suffers again and again on the altar as the Mass is held. As I said earlier, Charismatic leader Benny Hinn appears to believe the same thing. He stated "When you eat this bread you are eating the body of Jesus."

My own daughter, Julie, before she left the Roman Catholic Church, was a novitiate at several convents. She was training to become a nun. She has told me how the Host or circular wafer used in the mass was to be adored around the clock. There would be continual worship at the altar before the Host, with nuns taking turns to kneel and worship for an hour or more until someone came and took their place. (See below. Notice also the sunburst on the altar.)

Originally this belief was added to the early Church in order to placate the pagans and encourage them to enter the Roman Church. But it is nothing less than a blasphemous parody of pagan Rome, Egypt and Babylon cloaked in Christian words and phrases. This is so sad yet also so horrific. To believe the Lord Jesus Christ is contained in a box. To believe further that when the Host or wafer is placed on the altar during Mass Jesus is actually there, present, suffering. To believe that by performing good works and worshipping a circular wafer God will cleanse their sins.

This is little different from the sun worship we see portrayed in antiquity. In Babylon the sun was worshiped in the form of a sunburst, as it was also in ancient Egypt (see below).
Below on the left is the ancient worship of the sun god, transformed over the ages to represent the Lord Jesus Christ in the right hand photograph.

Who will tell these dear souls Christ died once and for all and took their sin once and for all time on the cross if they will but repent of their sins and trust in Him alone? Certainly those Protestant leaders wishing to join with Rome will not want to rock the boat by delivering such a devastating blow to one of Catholicism's central pillars of faith. No. They will keep quiet for the sake of unity and peace. And in doing so they will condemn others to a lost eternity in Hell for having believed a false Gospel and for having worshipped a false Jesus. A pagan divinity from Babylon now taking a central position within the Roman Catholic Superstate, the European Union, alongside his equally pagan mother "the Queen of Heaven."

"He who believes in the Son has everlasting life. He who does not believe the Son shall not see life, but the wrath of God abides on him" (John 3:36). We either believe in the Jesus of the

Bible who took all our sins on the cross or we do not. If you do not, you have followed a false Jesus. A Babylonian Jesus. An edible Jesus. And dear friends if you do not have the Jesus of the Bible, no matter how sincere you may be you will perish and go to Hell.

Julie would not listen to me. So I stayed in constant contact with her, prayed for her and showed her all my love. Then one day in the late 1990's God sent a lovely, gentle, Bible believing lady to the convent. Her task was to arrange the flowers etc. Whilst there the Lord told her to gently speak to the nuns about Jesus. Surprisingly most would not listen so she carried on her work and continued praying for them.

Then one day she chatted to Julie. All that I had said to Julie in the past suddenly began to germinate and bear fruit as this dear Christian explained the Gospel. The Holy Spirit gave light to Julie's soul and she did what men and women for centuries have done. She left the convent, followed Jesus and her life has totally changed. Julie could so easily have spent her life literally locked away from the world, worshipping a piece of bread and not the risen Saviour, the Jesus of the Bible. Thank God for that one faithful witness. How about you?

When a Catholic enters a Church he or she genuflects toward the altar. Because the Host is kept above the altar in what is known as the "Tabernacle" where the sunburst is displayed. To a Catholic mind the person genuflecting is bowing before JesusChrist. The Roman Catholic Church believes every time a Mass is held, the wafer (the Host) and the wine are changed into the very body and blood of the Lord Jesus Christ. Not this alone, but the Church also affirms that Christ is consciously present in the wafer and the wine. Through a change known as transubstantiation He is actually present, suffering on the altar every bit as much as He did on the cross. Several Catholic publications declare this blasphemy.

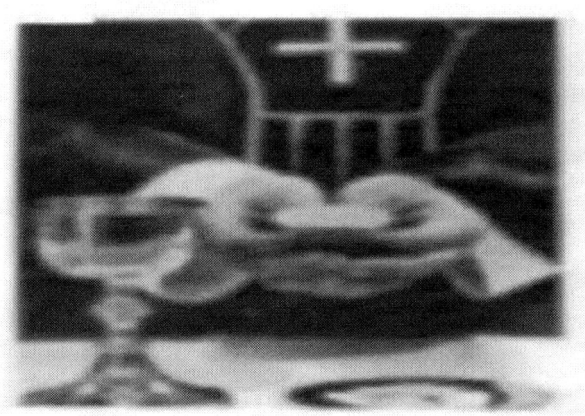

"The august sacrifice of the altar, then, is no mere empty commemoration of the passion and death of Jesus Christ, but a true and proper act of sacrifice whereby the high priest by an unbloody immolation offers himself a most acceptable victim to the eternal father, as he did on the cross" (34).

"In this divine sacrifice which is performed in the Mass, the very same Christ is contained and offered in bloodless manner who made a bloody sacrifice of himself once and for all on the cross. Hence the Holy Council teaches that it is a truly propitiatory sacrifice….." (35).

But what do the scriptures say? Heb. 9:24-28 states so clearly:

24 For Christ has not entered the holy places made with hands, which are copies of the true, but into Heaven itself now to appear in the presence of God for us;

25 <u>not that He should offer himself often</u>, as the high priest enters the Most Holy Place every year with the blood of another--

26 <u>He then would have had to suffer often</u> since the foundation of the world; but now, <u>once</u> at the end of the ages, He has appeared to put away sin by the sacrifice of Himself.

27 And as it is appointed unto men <u>once</u> to die, but after this the judgement,

28 <u>so Christ was offered once</u> to bear the sins of many………

Nothing could be clearer than this. Christ was offered once not many times. How many times do we die? Once. The book of Hebrews states *"as men die once….so Christ was offered once."* There is no need for Christ to be perpetually suffering on Catholic altars around the world. It is a lie. It is a blasphemy. It is a ceremony directed, not to the Jesus of the Bible, but to an ancient pagan sun god. There is no getting around this. Either we worship as the Bible prescribes or we worship in rebellion.

In the book of Exodus when the people of Israel rebelled at the foot of Mount Sinai, Aaron, the brother of Moses, fashioned a golden calf for the people to worship. What did Aaron say to them?

"Tomorrow shall be a feast to Jehovah." Exodus 32:5 (Original Hebrew).

Do you see? Even in their rebellion they thought they were worshipping Jehovah! How blind can one be? The same thing happened with the two sons of Aaron.

And Nadab and Abihu, the sons of Aaron, took either of them his censer, and put fire therein, and put incense thereon, and offered strange fire before the LORD, which he commanded them not. Leviticus 10:1.

Despite the fact that God had earlier given specific instructions on how He should be worshiped, even down to the ingredients for the incense to be used in the Tabernacle, Aaron's sons decided to create their own fire before the Lord. Notice they did it before the Lord. Not another god. How did God react? Did He commend them for their ingenuity in creating another form of worship? No. He destroyed them immediately. As Adam Clarke wrote in his excellent commentary on the Bible:

"...God intended that every part of his service should be conducted (in a certain manner); and that
every sacrifice might be acceptable to him, he sent
   his own fire as the emblem of his presence, and the
     means of consuming the sacrifice.--Here we find
Aaron's sons neglecting the divine ordinance, and offering incense with strange, that is, common fire, fire not of a celestial origin; and therefore the fire of God consumed them. So that very fire which, if properly applied, would have sanctified and consumed their gift,

become now the very instrument of their destruction! How true is the saying, "The Lord is a consuming fire!" He will either hallow or destroy us. He will purify our souls by the influence of His Spirit, or consume them with the breath of His mouth! ....Every part of the religion of God is divine. He alone knew what He designed by its rites and ceremonies, for that which they prefigured-- the whole economy of redemption by Christ-- was conceived in His own mind, and was out of the reach of human wisdom and conjecture. He therefore who altered any part of this representative system, who omitted or added anything, assumed a prerogative which belonged to God alone, and was certainly guilty of a very high offence against the wisdom, justice, and righteousness of his Maker.
This appears to have been the sin of Nadab and Abihu, and this at once shows the reason why they were so severely punished. The most awful judgments are threatened against those who either add to, or take away from, the declarations of God." See Deut. 4:2; Prov. 30:6; and Rev. 22:18-19 (Brackets added) (36).

Yet today we are expected to receive into our ranks a system of worship that totally denies the fact that Christ suffered once and once only. Instead we are expected to wink at the Roman Catholic form of worship which deceives its adherents into believing Christ is daily suffering on Catholic altars worldwide for the sins of mankind. And those who rush to join with Rome will tell you God is pleased with this ecumenical madness! If the words and the lessons given for our instruction in the Bible still have any relevance to the argument, He isn't pleased at all. In fact the joining with Rome will once again result in judgement upon rebellious people.

Chapter 7

Babylon comes to Rome

Semiramis was often portrayed with stars around her head. In many carvings and ancient paintings she is pictured holding the child Tammuz (Nimrod), the sun god, in her arms. The mother and child cult spread from Babylon to the nations where, even today, we see pictures and statues of the mother and child.

From Compton's Interactive Encyclopedia © 1999 The Learning Company, Inc.

In Egypt they were worshipped as Isis and her son Horus (see above). In India they were Shakti and Skanda. In Greece they were Aphrodite and Eros.

In Rome they became Venus and her son Cupid. In India, Assyria, Egypt, Greece, Rome, across the ancient world we find continuous references to the mother and child.

The king of Egypt, was known as Pharaoh. In Jeremiah 4:30 we read of Pharaoh Hophra. The name Hophra means priest. According to Young's Concordance of the Bible, the title Pharaoh means sun. So we are able to conclude Pharaoh Hophra was in fact priest of the sun. Or priest of the sun god. There is ample evidence to show the worship of Semiramis and Tammuz (Nimrod) the Mother and child, spread throughout the ancient world under different names. It came, at last, to Rome.

When the Emperor Constantine was converted, in what must be described as very questionable circumstances, he did not abolish the pagan religions of Rome. Instead he incorporated them into his version of Christianity. Much to the dismay of many believers who left Rome and became groups such as those mentioned earlier, who were persecuted by Rome before and after the Reformation. By the end of the 4th century, the Roman Catholic Church had begun to raise its head and within its walls were found many of the beliefs, customs and gods of Babylon. Now however they bore Christian titles and names.

ORIGIN	CHANGED TO:
PETA ROMA	PETER THE APOSTLE
FEAST OF SATURNALIA NIMROD (17-25 DEC)	CHRISTMAS PERIOD JESUS
DECEMBER 25 BIRTH OF THE SUN GOD	DECEMBER 25 BIRTH OF JESUS
SEMIRAMIS QUEEN OF HEAVEN	MARY QUEEN OF HEAVEN
VENUS AND CUPID	MARY AND JESUS
CROSSED KEYS OF JANUS	CROSSED KEYS OF PETER
CARDINALS OF JANUS	CARDINALS OF CHRIST
CAESAR PONTIFEX MAXIMUS	POPE PONTIFEX MAXIMUS

The Roman god, Peta Roma, who it was believed was the great interpreter of the mystery religions, was later Christianised and renamed the Apostle Peter. In ancient Rome the pagans celebrated the feast of Saturnalia in honour of the god Satur. It makes fascinating reading to discover the feast of Saturnalia was held during what is now known as the Christmas season. Between the dates of December 17 and 25 the ancients would send one another gifts. On 25 December they would celebrate the birth of Satur. Satur is merely another name for Nimrod or Tammuz the sun god, god of life and fertility.

The Roman Catholic Church merely changed the celebration of Satur's nativity into the nativity of the Lord Jesus. Many scholars would, today, place the birth of the Lord Jesus Christ around September/October during the feast of Tabernacles.

As we noted earlier, the Queen of Babylon, Semiramis was given the pagan title "Queen of Heaven." This title was later bestowed on Mary the mother of Jesus. Also, as we have noted, the mother and child of Roman paganism simply became Mary and Jesus of the Catholic Church. Next on our list we see the keys of the god Janus. They were crossed keys and were symbolic of the priests ability to permit or deny entry into the mystery religions of the time. The crossed keys to become the keys of Saint Peter often found in Roman Catholic imagery. Notice, also, the triple crown of the Pope previously worn by the Babylonian emperors.

The pagan religions even had a college of cardinals, as does Catholicism. Even the very title "cardinal" is taken from the pagans. According to the excellent book "Babylon The Great" written by Dr. Ian Sadler, the word is derived from the Latin "cardo" which means hinge. As possessors of the keys of Janus the cardinals were in effect the hinges which alone could swing open the doors of the mystery religions.

The pagan god Janus holding keys to the mystery religions

The crossed keys of the St. Peter and
The triple crown worn by the Pope and the kings of Babylon.

As has also been noted earlier, the Caesars held the title "Pontifex Maximus" high priest, or "chief bridge builder" between the gods and the people. Immediately upon the fall of Rome, the Pope took up the title as his own. Also, in Babylon, the religion of the god Dagon was popular. Dagon was a fish god often portrayed rising from the sea (Nimrod reborn). The priests of Dagon are portrayed wearing a mitre in the shape of a fish head with an open mouth. How absolutely astounding to discover the Pope and hierarchy of the Roman Catholic and Anglican Church sporting the same head wear.

Do you notice any similarity? They are virtually the same. The Babylonian religion of Nimrod and Semiramis became incorporated into the religion of ancient Rome.

Today the Pope carries a crosier. As you can see above, the priests of Dagon carried much the same implement. It was a rod for performing divination.

Further evidence for Rome being the inheritor of the Babylonian religion, is found in the name of the hill on which the Pope resides. Its name is Vaticanus. Translated it means "The place of divination." Roman Catholicism *is* the Babylonian religion disguised in Christian words and names. Nimrod became Tammuz the sun god. In effect the god of fire. One of the ways the ancients sought to reach perfection was through the cleansing fires of a halfway house to Heaven.

Many ancient religions believed you could pay to get your loved ones into Heaven. This is the same, in many respects, as the Roman Catholic Church's belief in the doctrine of Purgatory. A halfway house between Heaven and Hell.

Indulgences being sold in 16th Century Europe

Indulgences being sold by Buddhist monks

A place of incalculable suffering, where souls, through the fires of Purgatory, expunge the sins which were not atoned for by Christ's death on the cross. Instead of being saved completely by Christ's death on the cross, Catholics believe we must atone for some sins in the flames of Purgatory. A doctrine found nowhere in the accepted canon of scripture but found amply in ancient pagan beliefs and practices. Today, in the Roman Catholic Church, relatives of the dear departed still pay for prayers to be said in order for their loved ones to be gain an indulgence, an early release from this awful limbo. No one knows how many prayers are to be said or how many Masses must be performed in order to gain the release of souls from this fictitious prison. You could be there for thousands of years. Not even the Pope himself knows the length of time souls are required to suffer the most agonising torments within the flames of Purgatory before gaining entry into Heaven. Of course, one may completely bypass the flames of Purgatory through performing various deeds with the approval of the Church. If you are reading your Bible when you die you pass directly into Heaven. If you wear two small squares of cloth known as a scapular, the Virgin Mary has supposedly promised to come and personally take you from Purgatory to Heaven the first Saturday after your death. Ridiculous?

The man many Protestants believe to be an Evangelical, Pope John Paul II, has worn the scapular since he was a boy.

Enter any Catholic Church and you will eventually hear prayers being said for the dead. You can buy Mass cards for the dead containing a prayer for help, to Mary. But the Bible clearly states, as we have seen, that after death comes judgement. Prayers cannot help the soul that spent its entire earthly life ignoring the offer of Christ's substitutionary death on the cross. Your prayers cannot cause God to be more merciful to one who has placed his trust in the Lord Jesus alone and who has now died and entered His presence forever. Neither can your prayers gain entrance to Heaven for the soul that has not already placed its trust for forgiveness in the finished work of Christ on the cross. Once dead you are beyond the influence and aid of prayers uttered from this world or indeed the next.

Roman Catholic priest Martin Luther was moved to a righteous anger when the priest Tetzl travelled through 16th century Europe taking money from bereaved families on the pretext of freeing their loved ones from the pains of purgatory, or themselves, if the "indulgence" was bought in their own name. Tetzl's saying "The moment the coin in the coffer rings, the soul from Purgatory springs" was a demonic lie. The Lord Jesus Christ himself said the one who believes in Him and in the One who sent Him <u>has</u> everlasting life and <u>has</u> (not "will" but "has") passed from judgement into life (John 5:24). Was Jesus a liar or was he telling us the truth? Either the death of Christ was sufficient to save us from Hell or it was not. If it was, we need no purgatory.

If the death of Jesus Christ was not sufficient to save us, no amount of good works or suffering in this life or the life to come, offered by sinful hands to a pure and Holy God, will ever pay such an insurmountable debt. Salvation must be based upon the sinless Christ, not self. Scripture is crystal clear that it is all of Him and none of me. Yes, we perform good works once we have come to salvation. But our good works are a result of *being* saved, not an additional vehicle we use in order to *be* saved. Salvation in the New Testament is never presented as being available through Christ's death on the cross plus some undefined amount of work supplied by man. Such actions are an abominable affront to the very holiness and all sufficiency of the Son of God. However, the Roman Catholic religion teaches we must earn our salvation through good works.....

"It is a universally accepted dogma of the Catholic Church that man in union with the grace of the Holy Spirit must merit Heaven by his good works....we can actually merit Heaven as our reward...Heaven must be fought for; we have to earn Heaven"(37). Should you believe you are saved by faith in Christ's death and his death alone, then according to the Catholic Church, you are cursed. As the Council of Trent confirmed (1545-1563) "If anyone saith that justifying faith is nothing else but confidence in the Divine mercy which remits sin for Christ's sake alone; or, that this confidence alone is that whereby we are justified, let him be anathema (damned)"(38).

The much lauded Vatican II (1962-1965) is falsely believed to have brought a fresh breeze of biblical truth into the Vatican. It did not. Not one of the Council of Trent's curses has been amended. Pope John XXIII stated "I do accept entirely all that has been decided and declared at the Council of Trent." Trent's 100 plus curses against those who believe Christ's death was all sufficient still stand in Roman Catholic law. Friends, we join hands with Rome at our eternal peril! It is the descendant of the Babylonian and Roman Mystery religions, with a sprinkling of Christianity to give it an air of acceptability. Rome is the woman of Revelation 17. In the coming days she will not only ride and direct the Antichrist world government but will see to it that biblical Christianity is outlawed. May God open our eyes to see this before it is too late.

Chapter 8

ALL ROADS LEAD TO ROME

For centuries students of Bible prophecy have looked for and expected a revival of a political Roman Empire. But there is another power which has been with us since the fall of the Caesars. That power as we have seen is the Roman Catholic Church. In the coming days this power will, in many ways, control and direct the coming Antichrist empire until she herself is destroyed. The great World Religion she will yet evolve into as revealed in Revelation 17 and 18 is seen sitting astride revived political Rome. Directing her. Guiding her. She is, in embryonic form as yet. She will grow bolder still as the days progress.

Many saints of centuries gone by believed the Pope of Rome to be Antichrist or at least a type of Antichrist who would eventually become the ultimate Antichrist who would be destroyed by Christ at his coming. I cannot say the Pope will be *the* Antichrist. I cannot say he will not be. The Pope is said to be Christ's "vicar" on earth. In Christ's place. In Latin the title is "Vicarious Christi". In Greek it translates as "Antichrist". In this case it means in the place of Christ. Not against Christ.

Christians who were persecuted by Rome before the Reformation believed the Pope was an Antichrist. After the Reformation, men such as Luther; Calvin; John Knox; Zwingli; the Puritans; Wesley; Archbishop J.C.

Ryle; C.H. Spurgeon; Dr. Martin Lloyd-Jones and countless thousands of other Bible based saints, all believed the Pope of Rome to be an Antichrist. An Antichrist who would, possibly in the future, under a Revived Roman Empire, become the ultimate Antichrist. Or at very least head up the apostate religion that would become Babylon the Great.

Today we claim to honour these saints of days gone by. But we fail to listen to their warnings when it comes to Rome. We need to heed the words of these men.
To ignore their writings and especially the clear warnings of scripture, is an act of the utmost folly.

C.H. Spurgeon once wrote: "If one were to hand the text of Revelation 17 to a detective from Scotland Yard, he would immediately arrest the Church of Rome."

Imagine preaching the above words in most "Christian" circles today. If Spurgeon, that great preacher from the 19th century, were to return and preach these words in many Evangelical Churches today, he would be called a bigot and would be directed, unceremoniously, to the door. The Lord Jesus Christ said: *(You)* *"say, If we had been in the days of our fathers we would not have been partakers with them in the blood of the prophets"* (Matthew 23:30). Many today say "Oh, how I love the works of Spurgeon. I would have loved to have sat under and supported his ministry." Not so! Though many Christians honour men, such as Spurgeon, with their lips, their actions betray them. For the very things he and others stood against in their day, many are rushing to do today. Spurgeon, Whitefield, Wesley, Martin Lloyd-Jones and many other men of

God whose memory we claim to honour, would have stood and with trumpet like cries, denounced the lemming like rush back to Rome many have embarked upon in these last days. What blatant hypocrisy it is to claim to love the words of these saints of old, and yet betray their memory by your actions.

In 1887 Spurgeon stated: "Rather than be re-united with the idolatrous Church of Rome, I would rather see my own beloved Church perish and go to pieces. Rather than become Popish once more, she had better die" (39).

In our ecumenical climate today, where virtually any belief system is valid, to speak of the Pope and the Roman Catholic Church in such terms invites accusations of being "divisive, damaging to the work of God in bringing us into unity"; "divider of the brethren." Sadly, the truth of the matter is this. All too much of the teaching in many Churches today reveals a sad and in many cases spineless lack of solid, Bible based, doctrine. In the place of solid doctrine we find, a wishy-washy pandering to ecumenism, regardless of the patently obvious unscriptural teachings issuing from Rome.

In some Churches a love for Catholics has sprung up but its roots are placed in sentimentalism and not the word of God. God loves all men. But accepting men as they are is only the beginning not the end. True love will present the truth at any cost.

Even the cost of acceptance among ones peers. And there is only one truth, not many truths. Jesus said *"I am the way, the truth and the life. No man comes to the Father except through me."* (John 14:6). To say there are many truths, many paths to God, is to deny the clear statements of Jesus. If we do that we have no right to call ourselves his disciples. Yet many ignore the fact that Rome believes there are indeed many paths to God.

The teaching of many modern "ecumaniacs" flies in the face of past centuries filled with men and women who gave their lives to the study of the Bible. These people searched the scriptures. They believed they knew what they were talking about and were willing to die taking a stand against the errors and designs of Rome. To those who say "Let the Church be one" meaning "let us join with the Roman Catholic Church", may I offer you further words from the pen of Charles Spurgeon:

"(You say) 'The Church is one; woe to those who create division!' It does not matter that Mary is set up in the place of Christ, that images are worshipped, that rotten rags are adored, that pardons for every kind of crime are bought and sold..........Still you must 'keep the unity of the Spirit in the bond of peace.' You must lie down, restrain the testimony of the Spirit of God within you, keep His truth under a bushel and let the lie prevail."

Today the counter argument is heard "We have more light. The Catholic Church is simply another branch of Christianity." Not so. Historical evidence points to the Roman Catholic Church as the descendant of pagan religion and therefore not the true Christian religion. At best it is a sect. At worst it is the growing giant, Babylon the Great, that will engulf the earth, denying the Christ of the Bible and ultimately outlawing true Christianity that sees Jesus as the only way to God. The only way of salvation. The actions of Protestant, Evangelical Churches, bent on having ecumenical outreaches, dialogue with Eastern religions, "Churches together" and evangelistic co-operation with Rome, are merely a fulfilment of the words of the Lord Jesus and the Apostles of a falling away from the truth. A watering down of beliefs. And for what? For friendships sake. And this silence for friendships sake will be the eternal ruin of many. By not presenting the truth as revealed in scripture regarding salvation, many in the Ecumenical Movement etc. are taking souls to Hell with them.

All for the sake of misguided friendship. True friendship would warn of the errors of Rome and other religions that can damn a mans soul. True friendship would reach out and pull souls from the Hell they are running toward. Thank God for men with a fear of God in their hearts and a strong backbone of faith based on the truth of the Divine word of God Himself, coupled with a sincere love for the lost. All around us we see the prophesied falling away from the truth of the Bible. A falling away that will result in eternal ruin for many souls. Churches that adhere to the Bible will become havens for those who are escaping the great deception, the apostasy. The apostasy of the last days is not something future, my friends. It is here.

It is with us today.

Many of today's Church leaders are totally unaware, or are willingly ignorant, of the warnings of scripture and of saints from days gone by concerning the days in which we live. This joining with Rome will eventually play into the hands of Rome and her plans for a united Europe with a united religion under the Pope of Rome.

This is the plan. The death of Protestant Evangelicalism. The emergence of an all embracing, World Religion, based mainly in Rome. This religion will ride and influence the direction of the E.U. and the coming World Government in the not too distant future.

It has been said Pope John Paul II wishes to see Europe as it was before the Reformation. Yet men continue to exchange the truth for lies and lead their sheep into the lair of the wolf. Woe to the blind shepherds. What will they do when the Master returns and they realise their folly has cost the salvation of countless thousands of souls entrusted to their care? In your refusing to give the true Gospel to Rome you are condemning thousands to Hell for the sake of being their "friend". Some friend. To withhold the offer of salvation, all for the sake of a spurious unity.
Rome is wooing "separated brethren" from all
Christian denominations and from pagan religions
as we shall see later, to join her in her bed of apostasy.

On October 31, 1999, in Augsburg, Germany, the Roman Catholic Church and The Lutheran World Federation signed "The Joint Declaration on the Doctrine of Justification." The date on which they signed this document and overturned the Reformation was the anniversary of the day on which Luther posted his famous "95 Theses." Yet despite the Lutherans' declaration of unity with Rome, the Catholic Church continues to cling to the errors Luther and the reformers stood against.

In Britain, the Anglican and Roman Catholic Commission (ARCIC) made its Declaration on Justification in 1987. The Commission reached its climax in May 1999 when the "Final Report on Authority" called for complete surrender to the authority of the Papacy stating that should there ever be a One World Church, the Pope should be looked upon as supreme spiritual head.

In the early 1990's American Evangelical leaders and Roman Catholic leaders signed a document "Evangelicals and Catholics Together" announcing that Catholics are our brothers and sisters in Christ. Church leaders beware of the road you are taking.

The Church at large has been lulled to sleep by a Trojan horse that has been welcomed into the city of God. That Trojan horse is the Ecumenical Movement. Sadly, speaking as a Pentecostal, I have to include much in the Charismatic movement that has aided the deception in these days. Simply because someone professes to speak in tongues (or professes not to) is no passport to fellowship! An adherence to the word of God is the plumb line of acceptance into the fellowship of the saints. The Mormons believe in speaking in tongues. Yet they believe God, was once a man originating from a star system named Kolob! They also believe the Lord Jesus Christ and Satan are brothers, born as spirit beings when God had celestial sex with their mother! Totally blasphemous beliefs unsubstantiated by one word of scripture. Yet incredibly, the Mormons were invited to join the "March for Jesus" in the U.S.A. in 1999 in Salt Lake City, Utah. On the day of the March, local organiser Maggy Fletcher said: "Over a dozen Churches of various denominations are directly involved with the march, but many more Churches have shown an interest in coming . . . Lutherans, Catholics, Methodists, Presbyterians, Baptists, Episcopalians, Assembly of God, non-denominational, Charismatics (and) LDS [Mormon]." She said that though the Church of Jesus Christ of Latter-day Saints has not endorsed the event, individual Mormons have expressed interest in participating "and are welcome to do so" (40). According to Maggy Fletcher, Mormons would appear to be part of the "body of Christ." She said "The March for Jesus unites believers, regardless of colour, race or denominations, into the Body of Christ. The names on the Church buildings don't mean a thing" (41).

The U.S. national coordinator of March for Jesus, Tom Pelton, agreed with Maggy Fletcher's sentiments, saying, "It's time to move beyond Church walls to connect with one another and the community" (42).

Many of us would say it is totally unacceptable to allow a cult, such as the Latter Day Saints with their unscriptural beliefs, to join a "March for Jesus" rally. However, sad to say, even the much praised "March for Jesus" would appear to promote an unscriptural agenda.

Many Christians believe the aim of the march is to be a witness to the unchurched in our area. We will see this is not the intention of the organisers. Also while I am all for Christians getting together as a witness to the Gospel I have never heard a full Gospel message preached at a "March for Jesus" though I have not attended every one. I have heard a "come to Jesus and get a better life" Gospel. Which is not the Gospel as presented in the Bible. The Bible presents man as a total rebel against God. A lawbreaker. As someone who is dead as far as spiritual things are concerned. Yet the Gospel I hear today is one of our being incomplete without God. I hear stories on how He longs to make us happy, otherwise we shall finish our lives in a "Christless eternity." While it is true that God wants us to be whole, happy and totally fulfilled, this is not the Gospel. The Gospel truth is this, man is a rebel on his way to judgement and Hell. He is in a terrifying position, standing condemned already by his lifestyle and inherent sinfulness. No amount of good works can save him because his good works are still offered by sinful, guilty hands. To break just one of the laws of God is enough to condemn a man for eternity. Not to a politically correct "Christless eternity" which could mean anything. If you have lived a Christless life why fear a Christless eternity? The term means nothing to most non-Christians.

The truth is at the moment of death the unrepentant man or woman will be sent to Hell itself. A terrifying place of unimaginable conscious horror, where they will stay forever. But by dying on the cross, Jesus Christ, the only pure man to have ever lived, took upon himself our punishment. In an awesome act of mercy toward the guilty, God treated Jesus as if he were you (guilty, sinful and condemned) in order that He could treat you as if you were Jesus (pure, innocent and holy). He stood in your place and mine, suffering the full force of God's anger. He willingly took the judgement that should have been poured out on us. As a result of that incredible sacrifice by Christ, all those who turn from their sin (rebellion against God) and follow Him alone and trust in His sacrifice alone for their pardon will be saved. All those who will not must suffer their own punishment because they have rejected God's free offer of forgiveness offered by Christ. That is the Gospel. Yet today we are sold a cheap salvation based on a "feeling good about ourselves" experience. And it is a lie. A deception from the pit.

The leaders of "March for Jesus" Graham Kendrick, Gerald Coates, Roger Forster and others, though sincere, are, I believe, unscriptural in their agenda. While many of those participating may be true Christians they are totally misinformed as to the true reason for the march. Graham Kendrick has gone on record stating "…direct evangelism has never been the primary purpose for the marches." Then what is the main thrust of the March for Jesus? The organisers believe as they march they are "shifting the spiritual powers that have been allocated in the structure of the nations"(43). Sounds so good doesn't it? What a shame Jesus and the Apostles didn't know this neat trick for pushing the Church forward. For instance Paul could have avoided being stoned, shipwrecked, beaten, whipped and so on if only he had realised this amazing secret for winning souls instead of preaching the uncompromising truth. Just march and dislodge those pesky spiritual beings that rule over nations. Then you can move in, preach a "God loves you and wants you to be fulfilled" Gospel and the world will belong to us. Now it sounds silly doesn't it? And it is. Actually the Bible says nothing about marching and shifting "territorial spirits" at all. The fact that these men are able to foist their teaching on the Church is simply because the Church has forgotten how to study the word of God and spot false teaching.

False teaching which, just a few years ago, would have been easily identified by a child of 10. But this glut of false teachers was predicted by our Lord and the Apostles. False shepherds, false prophets and the professing Church, in these last days, loves to receive this teaching which comes directly out of the Occult and "New Age". However, as we shall see, the Roman Catholic Church has equally, and worse, unscriptural beliefs and we are expected to join with them. In fact just a short time ago I witnessed the leaders from my old Charismatic Church marching with the Catholic Church down our main street observing the Stations of the Cross.

Something the lead elder intimated he would never do. But there he was.

This is the path on which so many, once solid Churches, are embarking. The path back to Rome. So many are blissfully unaware of Rome's strategy for Christendom, Europe and the world. So sleepy they do not notice where their leaders are taking them. Just lay back and enjoy the teaching. Above all do not question it. Rome is our friend. Let's all climb in bed together.

Sleep and wait for the Second Coming. But please do not ask me to think, pray, question and study. Friend, climbing into bed with Rome will unite you with lovers your Christian forefathers would never have believed possible.

In the next chapter we shall look at just a few of Rome's many lovers.

Chapter 9

THE WHORE AND HER LOVERS

Pope John Paul II has travelled the entire planet in his ecumenical quest to bring all religions together under Rome. It is clear from his teachings and statements he accepts the validity of all belief systems.

Sri Chinmoy is known as the Hindu guru of the U N, where he holds regular classes in meditation. His 80 plus meditation centres around the world promote the Antichristian belief in Hindu deities. Yet Pope John Paul II told him "The Hindu life and the Christian life shall go together. Your message and my message are the same."(44) Evangelical leaders, conducting "Churches Together" and "Evangelistic" outreach meetings with the Roman Catholic Church, may I ask you, is your message the same as the Hindu message? If not then why are you in bed with Rome? Do not bury your head in the sand and pretend your union with Rome is different from the union revealed within these pages. It is not. It matters not if it is Islam; Animism; Zoroastrianism; Shamanism; Voodoo; Spiritism; Hinduism; Buddhism; New Age techniques; Evolution. The Roman Catholic Church and the Pope are scouring the world in an attempt to bring all religions, all belief systems into the halls of the Roman Catholic Church. The Catholic Church is telling the followers of these false religions "You can follow these beliefs and still be partners with us." Christian leaders by your joining with

Rome you are condoning this affront to the validity and uniqueness of the word of God. God will not hold you guiltless. Indeed many of Rome's adherents have no knowledge of the Vatican aims and dreams for humanity. Those who do are keeping as quiet as possible until it is too late to protest. One of the Pope's closest friends is the Dalai Lama of Tibet, who believes in reincarnation and thinks he is a god. The Dalai Lama has even preached in St. Pierre Cathedral in Geneva, Switzerland. The former Church of John Calvin.

The Cathedral's dean, William McComish, called the Dalai Lama "His Holiness".

McComish stated that "the Cathedral was now becoming a home for a new religious centre to experience understanding between the world's major faiths". This "understanding" will play right into the plans of Rome. The Pope holds regular ecumenical meetings at the Vatican, playing host to all manner of faiths both weird and blasphemous.

Is it possible the Apostles would have played host to the pagan faiths of the ancient world in an effort to gain "greater understanding and co-operation between all faiths"? Absolutely not. Although they had many an opportunity to have "dialogue" with the non-Christian religions around them, the Apostles were continually challenging false belief systems with the facts concerning the life, death, burial, resurrection and ascension of the Messiah. They also warned of coming judgement. Not so Rome. When the Pope visited Egypt in 2000 some of his opening words were "I have not come to preach the Gospel." One wonders if John Paul

II is even aware of the true Gospel. Or perhaps Jesus and the Apostles got it wrong. Maybe Jesus should have attempted to have dialogue with the scribes and the Pharisees instead of calling them "whitewashed sepulchres." Perhaps Paul should have sat down with the Jews and the Greeks of his day and attempted to see the "Divine" in them and let them believe what they wanted. No, Jesus, the Apostles, all of them, knew that to keep the truth to themselves would result in their hearers going to Hell.

At this point I feel it right to state, as I did at the beginning, I am not writing this book simply to create controversy. I am writing it out of a sincere concern for all men and women in these last days prior to the return of the Lord Jesus. The prophecies of the Bible have yet to be shown to have failed in any point. If that is so then soon a false world Church will arise as the prophets said. It will lead mankind away from, not to, the truth. I am certain, as were countless believers before me, the Roman Catholic Church will spearhead, or at the very least be incredibly instrumental, in that world Church. Past and present events would indicate this to be true. Therefore to have anything to do with Rome is to enter a liaison, which will result in judgement of the utmost severity. Should we, who study the prophecies of the Bible, remain silent while prophetic events overtake us until we are no longer permitted by law to present the truth as revealed in the scripture?

Only the true faith as presented by Jesus and the Apostles can save the multitudes of men and women who are caught up in false religious systems. They are either presented with a totally false view of the Bible or are trapped in a never ending round of good works. Good works are fine but they are useless when used by sinful men in an effort to appease a Holy God. The problem is, not even the Pope himself can tell you how many good works are sufficient to gain entry into Heaven. The wonderful truth is Christ totally paid the penalty for your sins when He died on the cross of Calvary.

Salvation is free to you and me. But it cost God the death of His own Son in our place. This is the glorious truth Rome keeps from her subjects. Her view of salvation is Christ's death plus some undetermined amount of works as we have already seen, followed by undetermined ages being tormented in Purgatory in order to purge away the sins not cleansed by Christ. But that is a satanic lie to keep us in bondage. Christ died to set us free without works (Eph. 2:8,9). Works are a result of *being* saved. Not a bribe offered to God in order to get Him to turn a blind eye to our sins. Christ plus works is a false Gospel. It is a lie. Yet there are those dear beloved souls within the Catholic Church who believe in Christ alone to save them without works or ritual. We on the outside must encourage our brothers and sisters in their work for the Lord within the Catholic Church. But we must be under no illusion the day is approaching when they must come out and leave the Church and the people they have grown to love. Most ordinary Catholics are sincere people who have been brought up in the Church and so know nothing else but that which they have been taught from childhood. We must show love and compassion toward them while at the same time gently presenting them with the truth from scripture, praying that God will be pleased to give them light and lead them away from error to truth. We must also understand that when one has been taught error from childhood, by those one trusts i.e. the priests, nuns and leaders of the Church, who probably know no better than those they teach, it is most difficult and painful to acknowledge one has been schooled in error and to tear oneself away from those whom one has come to love and respect. Any Protestants who have been sold the lie over the "Toronto blessing", so called, and other false teaching and have woken to discover ones leaders have been teaching dangerous, unscriptural nonsense will agree it is so painful to walk away from a fellowship one has come to love and trust. How much harder, then, for one schooled from childhood in Catholic doctrine to be suddenly brought into the glare of scriptural truth as opposed to Catholic error. Only a sovereign act of God can free these dear ones.

We must show love to all who are caught up in unscriptural organisations. There, but for the grace of God, go you and I.

In Assisi Italy in 1986 Pope John Paul II met with the Dalai Lama, Orthodox Christians, the Archbishop of Canterbury, as well as many from various pagan beliefs including Indian Shamen, Buddhist monks, Animists.

During this ecumenical gathering at the Church of Assisi the gods of other religions were placed in a position of high honour on the altar of this professedly "Christian" Church.

It is worth noting that just a few short years later the same Church was destroyed by an earthquake. But are we listening? It would appear not. In 1992 the Roman Catholic Church held yet another all embracing ecumenical conference in Assisi.

It would never surprise me to find that when Antichrist enters the Temple in Jerusalem it will be a Temple not for Jews only but will become a place for all nations, all faiths. Pagan edifices could be placed in parts of the Temple while other faiths place their deities in adjacent areas. More on this point later.

It was very interesting to note that as the 20th century drew to a close and Pope John Paul II prepared to make his historic pilgrimage to Israel, he stated to astounded advisors 'There is no reason why the Vatican has to be in Rome alone." He then went even further and said "I am looking forward to visiting Jerusalem, my second Vatican." Many believe the Vatican made an agreement with Israel under former Prime Minister Shimon Peres and the Palestinian Authority under Yasser Arafat, to recognise the Palestinians right to Jerusalem. The plan, drawn up in the early 1990's before the Oslo agreement, is to make Jerusalem both the capital of Israel and a Palestinian state. French intellectual and close friend of Peres, Mark Halter stated that he had personally handed a letter from Peres to the Pope in 1994 offering the Vatican sovereignty over Jerusalem's Old City. This plan is ongoing. The same powerful men who produced the Oslo agreements are the same men who penned the Peres plan and wish to bring in a World Government. The idea behind the Oslo accords etc is not to bring peace but intensified conflict to the Middle East resulting in calls for an international presence in

Jerusalem. Without conflict it is so much harder for the powerbrokers promoting the New World Order to exert control over the nations they wish to draw in to a One World Government and One World Religion.

First you use deceptive means to intensify the conflict such as include the demand that the Palestinians must be armed. This was one of the Oslo terms, which Israel followed. Then when all Hell breaks out you move your choice men and organisations into the area in order to bring "peace" and prepare that particular country for a World Government. The Vatican and the United Nations are poised to be that presence in the Middle East and Jerusalem. The Pope has also stated he would be prepared to be the head of the World Council of Churches if it were based in Jerusalem. To have the Pope of Rome overseeing the WCC from both Rome and Jerusalem would be of tremendous prophetic significance. Especially when one realises that all manner of beliefs are welcomed in the WCC. And the Pope wants to oversee the whole organisation. Within the WCC one discovers among its members some Christians who long to see true understanding and brotherhood between all who truly profess Christ as Lord. Also some members are pagan and some blatantly apostate and perverse.

Simply as examples, in November 1993, the World Council of Churches sponsored a Re-imaging conference in Minneapolis, Minnesota attended by almost 2,000 "Christian" women. One such attendee and speaker was Delores Williams of Union Theological Seminary, who, during a debate said: 'I don't' think we need a theory of atonement at all. I think Jesus came for life and to show us something about life. I don't think we need folks hanging on crosses and blood dripping and weird stuff." The idea of "folks hanging on crosses" appears to be an affront to Ms. Williams. She doesn't even feel we need a "theory of atonement." One might well wonder what this representative of Union Theological Seminary believes regarding salvation itself. Remember this is, supposedly, a Christian" speaker. Someone who was representing a Christian Seminary. Someone who presumably believes we can all get to Heaven without the cross of Christ. This woman had the effrontery to teach others that we do not need Jesus Christ except as a guide to teach us "something about life." What that "something" is Ms. Williams apparently doesn't expand upon. But the damage is already done. She is leading her hearers away from the truth of the Gospel.

At the WCC sponsored conference other speakers included: Virginia Mollenkott, a pro-abortion lesbian who participated in the translation of the New International Version of the Bible. During her lecture Ms. Mollenkott stated that because the Lord Jesus went to the cross and suffered in obedience to the Father, God the Father was an abusive parent.

Another speaker, Nadean Bishop, was the first openly lesbian called to minister in an American Baptist Church. During her message to the conference Bishop said the sisters of Lazarus, Mary and Martha were not sisters, but lesbian lovers.

Janie Spahr, a lesbian clergywoman in the Presbyterian Church of America stated she found her theology through "making love with Coni," her lesbian partner.

During the conference, a group of roughly 100 "lesbian, bi-sexual, and transsexual women" gathered on the platform and were given a standing ovation by many in the crowd. They were "celebrating the miracle of being lesbian, out, and Christian."

Unbelievably on the Sunday of the conference the women joined together in a shamelessly indecent prayer to the heathen goddess Sophia,

"Our maker Sophia, we are women in your image. ... Sophia, creator God ... shower us with your love. ... we invite a lover, we birth a child; with our warm body fluids we remind the world of its pleasures and sensations. . . Our guide, Sophia, we are women in your image."

It truly boggles the mind when one realises that what we are reading about is a "Christian" gathering. And some have the blindness of mind to say "The apostasy is something way in the future."

The goddess Sophia is usually depicted as a bare breasted, balding woman with a pagan "Tika" or "Talik" sign on her forehead. The sign is in the form of a red dot, worn by Hindu worshippers. Surely the Pope as a "Christian" leader would never countenance the wearing of a sign in honour of a pagan goddess. Would he?

Below, you can see the answer to the question. Pope John Paul II, in his eagerness to embrace all faiths under Rome, is pictured receiving the "Talik" from a pagan priestess.

At the WCC assembly in Canberra in 1991, Chung Hyun Kyung, Professor of Theology at Ewha Women's University of Seoul, invoked the spirits of those who had suffered injustice. She included the spirits of Bible characters such as Hagar, Uriah, the daughter of Jephthah and the infants murdered by King Herod. She also summoned the spirits of Mahatma Ghandi, Steve Biko, Martin Luther King Jr. and Victor Jara. She moved on to call up the spirits of the Amazon rain forest, air, earth and water, raped, tortured and exploited by the human greed for money. She finally summoned Jesus. "Come. The spirit of the liberator, our brother Jesus, tortured and killed on the cross." (45) This is so anti biblical it barely needs mentioning. To summon the spirits of the dead is an abomination to God and strictly forbidden (Deut. 18:10-12). Also notice, the Lord Jesus Christ is merely a liberator tortured and killed on the cross. Not the Lord who rose from the tomb having conquered sin, death and the devil. His uniqueness is devalued by those professing to be His disciples. Naturally many Bible believers within the W.C.C. are very disturbed by the route the W.C.C. has decided to take and may almost certainly be forced, by their consciences, to leave this hypocritical organisation masquerading as a Christian body. And this is the organisation the ecumenical all embracing Pope of Rome wishes to oversee from Jerusalem. One may argue as much as one likes but the facts reveal quite clearly the Roman Catholic Church to be the offspring of pagan Rome and the ancient Babylonian religion with plans for all to join her on her journey to Hell.

Throughout this book I have attempted to show some of the more glaring anti-scriptural beliefs held by Rome. One of the most obvious is the belief that all men of good will get to Heaven regardless of whether or not they believe Jesus Christ died in their place. Some may argue, despite what has been said in previous pages, that Roman Catholicism is Christian. In 1994 the Church published the latest Catechism. Here is what it states regarding other faiths.

"Those who through no fault of their own, do not know the Gospel of Christ or His Church, but who nevertheless seek God with a sincere heart, and, moved by grace, try in their actions to do His will as they know it through the dictates of their conscience --- those too may obtain salvation." (46)

With regard to Islam the Catechism makes special mention:

"The plan of salvation also includes those who acknowledge the Creator, in the first place amongst whom are the Muslims; these profess to hold the faith of Abraham, and together with us they adore the one, merciful God, mankind's judge on the last day."(47)

What we find contained in the above two statements is a denial of the Gospel. First, what man has a "sincere heart"? The Bible says *"The heart is deceitful above all things and desperately wicked. Who can know it?"* (Jer. 17:9).

The only way for a heart to be changed is by Jesus Christ performing a miracle when a man hears and, by the moving of the Holy Spirit, responds to the good news of God's forgiveness through Christ's atoning death. At that moment, through the regenerating power of the Holy Spirit, he can be changed forever. If a man never hears the message of Christ he can never come to salvation regardless of how sincere he may be.

Secondly, the god of Islam is not the God of Abraham and the Bible. Anyone who cares to study Islam soon discovers that in opposition to the message of love and forgiveness found in the Jewish Bible, Islam is a religion of intolerance and war. The very word Islam means submission. According to Islamic teaching all humanity belong to one of two houses. Dar'as'salaam, the house of peace or Dar'al'harrb, the house of war. The house of peace includes all who embrace Islam. The house of war relates to all who refuse Islamic teaching. Both houses will continue to be at war until the house of peace conquers the house of war bringing all men under submission to Allah. Mohammed planned and participated in many bloody wars designed to subjugate nations to Islam. The terrorists who ploughed planes into the New York World Trade Centre on September 11th 2001 cannot be considered Islamic extremists any more than George Whitefield or John and Charles Wesley can be considered Christian extremists. These Christian evangelists believed the Bible to be true and as such followed literally its commands to preach the Gospel. So do Islamic "extremists." When the Bible says "Go into all the world and preach the Gospel" these men and countless others willingly obeyed. When the Koran exhorts Muslims to kill the unbeliever they too, obey its commands.

Those who proclaim Allah to be simply another name for the God of the Bible are misleading their hearers. Allah was simply the name of one of 360 desert, tribal gods. When Mohammed and his followers first arrived in Mecca they destroyed all the tribal gods but one, Allah. Allah was the god of the moon. This is the reason one sees a crescent moon on the minarets of Islamic Mosques.

According to Arabian legend Allah, the moon god, was married to the Sun goddess. Together, Allah and his wife produced three daughters, Manat, Al-Lat and

Al-Uzza. Also, Allah is not simply another word for God. The actual Arabic word for God or "the Lord" is Al-Rabb (pronounced Al-Rubb). Those who tell you Allah is another name for the God of the Bible are either uninformed or lying. <u>Allah is a personal name not a title</u>. The God of Israel has a personal name. Yahweh or, as it was westernised by a Catholic priest in the 13th Century, Jehovah. Furthermore Allah and the God of the Bible couldn't be further apart when it comes to the subject of Jesus Christ. The God of the Bible has a son, Jesus Christ, the Messiah of Israel and Saviour of the world. What does the Koran have to say about God having a Son?

"O people of the Scripture! Do not exaggerate in your religion nor utter aught concerning Allah save the truth. The Messiah, Jesus son of Mary, was only a messenger of Allah, and His word which he conveyed unto Mary, and a spirit [sic.] from Him. So believe in Allah and His messengers and say not 'Three' - Cease! It is better for you! -Allah is only one God. Far is it removed from His transcendent majesty that He should have a son ...The Messiah will never scorn to be a slave unto Allah". (Sura 19:35).

This being so, why does the Catholic Church have the effrontery to proclaim the God of the Bible to be one and the same as the god of Islam? The obvious answer is because Rome wants all faiths under her wing and is willing to hide the truth behind an ecumenical façade. Also conveniently ignored is the fact that over 250,000, Christians are martyred every year and most of them meet their deaths in Muslim countries. As Rev. David Pawson states, that means roughly 3,000 Christian martyrs every 4 days. A little more than the number of deaths in the World Trade Centre tragedy. The West went to war over those deaths. But little is said of those thousands of Christians who perish each year at the hands of the followers of Islam. British Prime Minister Tony Blair and American President George Bush have painted Islam as a peace loving religion. While many Muslims do wish to live in peace, a vast number believe a peaceful world will emerge only when the entire planet is submitted to Allah and Islam. Until then Islam is at war.

Christians need to wake up to the fact that in 2001 an estimated 25,000 people converted to Islam. We are not speaking of conversions in the Far East or even the Middle East. No.

THESE PEOPLE WERE CONVERTED IN THE UNITED KINGDOM!

We can but recommend the excellent teaching video by David Pawson titled
THE CHALLENGE OF ISLAM TO CHRISTIANS. Available from Anchor Recordings, Kent. England.

With regard to Rome's acceptance of other faiths, I have a Catholic booklet in my possession titled "Can Only Christians Be Saved?" According to the teaching of this small booklet, the answer is no. Apparently even if you are an atheist but try to do your best in life, you will be saved because you are being saved by the "invisible Christ." So every man or woman of "good will" will get to Heaven regardless of whether or not they believe in Jesus. One of the front runners for the position of Pope, is the very influential Cardinal Francis

Arinze who oversees the dialogue between Rome and Islam. Should he ever become Pope, Arinze would be a powerful link between Rome and the religion of Mohammed. In an interview in 1999, he was asked "Can only Christians get to Heaven?" Arinze responded, "If a person were to push what you said a little further and say that if you're not a Christian you're not going to Heaven, we'd regard that person as a fundamentalist, and theologically wrong. I met in Pakistan a Muslim. He had a wonderful concept of the Koran. We were like two twins that had known one another from birth. And I was in admiration of man's wisdom. I think that man will go to Heaven. There was a Buddhist in Kyoto, in Japan. This man, a good man, open listening, humble--I was amazed. I listened to this man's words of wisdom and said to myself, "The grace of God is working in this man." The interviewer then repeated the question, "So you can still get to Heaven without accepting Jesus?" "Expressly, yes (he laughs with the audience)." (Dallas Morning News, 20/3/99). So not only do Catholic booklets and even the Catholic Catechism tell us we do not need to accept Jesus in order to get to Heaven, but Protestant Christian leaders continue to seek ways to return themselves and their Churches to heathen Rome.

Shortly before the turn of the century the Pope was visited by a delegation of Muslim clerics from Iran. The gift they brought was the Koran which states *"Allah is only one God. Far is it removed from His transcendent majesty that He should have a son"* (Sura 19:35). As we have seen this is an outright denial of the Divine Sonship of Jesus Christ. How did the Pope receive this gift? Pope John Paul II dutifully bowed to the book and kissed the front cover in homage. He paid homage to a book which totally denies the Christian faith when it states, "God has no Son."

But the idea of a universal salvation for all faiths is not confined to Rome. Even Charismatic leader, writer and author of the Alpha Course, Nicky Gumbel, would appear to believe sincerity is enough to gain salvation. In his new booklet "What About Other Religions" Gumbel, after stating on page 13 that "it is illogical to assert that all religions are equally true or that all religions lead to God" goes on to say on page 16 "..it is possible for someone to be saved by faith through grace even if they have never heard of Jesus." Gumbel cites Abraham, David and the tax collector who were justified by faith even though they had never heard of Jesus. The problem with this kind of thinking is this. The men cited were all Jews who believed in the one true God who revealed Himself to Israel alone. Furthermore they looked to Him alone to justify them. They were not following Baal or Ashteroth, Allah, Molech or any other false god. The Bible never gives the slightest hint that anyone following pagan beliefs will be saved if they are sincere enough. Mr. Gumbel seems to believe that these also may find salvation so long as they are sincere. So in his eyes it doesn't matter what you believe as long as you are kind, sincere and seek to do good to all men. He affirms Jesus is the only Saviour, of course, but he seems to be saying if you are worshipping Diva or the Buddha or whatever, as long as you seek God, (large G or little g), with a sincere heart you will be saved. What does the scripture say? Scripture alone, not Mr. Gumbel or the Pope, must be our only guide.

In the book of Exodus the Jews were warned by the Lord not to have anything to do with the gods of the other nations. Surely if we follow the presumed reasoning of Nicky Gumbel why should mixing with those of other beliefs be a problem? As long as they are sincere and nice people they too may obtain salvation.

Why did the Lord Jesus Christ say to the Jews of His day *"If you do not believe I am He you will die in your sins"* (John 8:24)? Because you must believe in the Lord Jesus Christ in order to be saved. Sincerity is not enough. I am sure the retort might be "How about Romans 10:12 *"For there is no distinction between Jew and Greek, for the same Lord over all is rich to all who call upon Him."* Surely this means any who seek God sincerely through their religion will be saved?" But many who may quote this verse in defence of Gumbel and his colleagues who believe the same thing miss the point Paul is making. Paul is saying you shall be saved if you call on *"the Name of the Lord"* not Allah or Rama or some other deity.

No matter how sincere you are you need to hear and receive the Gospel of Jesus Christ in order to be saved. Paul puts the question in verse 14 of Romans chapter 10. How can anyone call upon the Lord, the one true God of Israel, unless he has heard the message through the preaching of the word of God? Yet it seems Nicky Gumbel, the Vatican and the foolish, weak and rebellious Protestant Evangelical leaders would like to see us all in a melting pot of faiths. "Yes" they say "Jesus is the only way; Christianity is the true religion but if you are in another belief system and you are sincere you too may find salvation." Blind leaders of the blind, all shall fall into the pit.

Concerning the Jewish people we all know that for the most part they do not believe the Lord Jesus Christ was the promised Messiah. They are expecting someone other than Jesus to come as the long awaited deliverer of Israel. It would seem the Catholic Church agrees with them. In July 2002 the Roman Catholic Church stated the Jewish people are theologically correct in expecting their Messiah. It is difficult to take on board the enormity of this statement. The Roman Catholic Church is saying the Jewish people, who in the main reject Jesus Christ, are in fact correct in looking to a future Messiah.

To add to the Roman Catholic Church's crime of denying the legitimacy of Christ's claim to be Israel's one and only Messiah when He came 2000 years ago, in August 2002 a conference of American Catholic Bishops went further and issued a document which stated that to target Jews for evangelisation is not acceptable. Why? The document states "..Jews already dwell in a saving covenant with God."

The document continues "Jews are also called to prepare the world for God's Kingdom." So according to Rome the Jewish people are right to look for a coming Messiah and we are not to evangelise them because they are already in a saving covenant with God and are preparing the world for His coming Kingdom. In that case who will the Jewish nation accept as the Messiah instead of the Lord Jesus Christ? Why, the coming false Messiah of the last days of course. I wonder, could it be as our departed Christian brothers believed centuries ago? Could the coming Antichrist when he appears turn out to be the Pope of Rome? A Pope possibly of Jewish origin? Or one who is influential within the Mosques of Islam? Or will the Antichrist be a great political leader whom the Pontiff will point to as the great deliverer from the problems of the Middle East and the rest of the world? The future European and hence world leader? Should the Pope lead the world to follow this coming monster he would then very easily slip into the shoes of the prophesied "False Prophet" of Revelation 13 and 19:20 who will rule alongside the Antichrist.

As we gaze into the mist obscuring the coming days, we cannot see clearly. But soon all will become as the noonday. Then beware of this coming deliverer as he proclaims himself to be a god in the newly built Temple in Jerusalem (2 Thess. 2:3,4) and suddenly turns on the Jewish people and all those who believe in the God of Israel and His true Messiah, Jesus Christ. It would appear from the statements issuing from the Vatican and ecumenical, Charismatic and other Church leaders, many are being prepared for the appearance of the man of sin, the Antichrist and his number two, the False Prophet.

Rome has dialogue with all and sundry in an effort to spread her net around the globe, influencing world events, religions and governments. She gazes with expectancy toward the time when a World Government will make its appearance on the world stage. On that day Rome will be ready. Her work behind the scenes complete she will take centre stage fully prepared to guide and counsel the kingdom of the Antichrist, be he Pope or politician, and become the home of men of good will from all faiths and even those who have no faith at all. Religious Rome will lie and tell them "All is well. We are all on the road to Heaven together." The Bible will become just another sacred book of spiritual truth alongside the Koran; the Bhagavad Gita; the Book of Mormon and so on. A real melting pot of beliefs. And from this mixture will emerge the One World Religion destined to sit beside Antichrist. Deceiving the entire globe into believing God is pleased with them and displeased with the Christian fundamentalists who must be outlawed and the land grabbing Jews who must be stamped out. Reader take care you are not found to be on the wrong side when God arises to judge the earth in the not too distant future. As we shall see in the next chapter, one of the aces up the ecumenical sleeve of the Vatican is the growing cult of the Virgin Mary, with followers from around the planet. From all religions, especially "Christian" and Muslim.

Chapter 10

MARY THE MOTHER GODDESS AND THE NEW WORLD RELIGION

In this chapter we shall look at the Virgin Mary of the Catholic Church, her influence on the Pope, the Catholic laity and those of other faiths. We shall also compare her with the Virgin Mary of the Bible. I believe we shall unearth some disturbing facts, which in turn will raise some equally disturbing questions. Not least, questions regarding her role in the current and future European empire and the coming false One World Religion. Pope John Paul II has dedicated his entire Pontificate, not to God or the Lord Jesus Christ, but to Mary. His motto is "Totus Tuus", "totally yours, Mary." He is especially dedicated to the cult of Our Lady of Fatima. In 1917 three children at Fatima in Portugal, began to have visions of what they believed was the Virgin Mary. This occurred on the 13th of May 1917.

Exactly 65 years later on May 13th 1981 Pope John Paul II narrowly missed two bullets from a would be assassin as he bent to inspect a child's medal of Our Lady of Fatima. Even though he was hit by a third bullet, he believes the Virgin Mary saved his life. Following that event and a subsequent private message from the Virgin, the Pope has dedicated all of Russia to the Virgin Mary as was requested by the supposed vision in 1917. Please tell me, is this the Christian faith of the Bible or are we dealing with something more sinister?

Pope John Paul II bowing in adoration before a statue of Mary.

Certainly many would look on the adoration of Mary as pure pagan superstition stemming from the ancient prayers to Semiramis, Queen of Heaven and the worship of her son Tammuz (Nimrod) the sun god. The adoration of the Virgin Mary has grown to incredible proportions with literally millions flocking to apparition sites and Marian shrines each year in order to gain some favour from the Virgin or simply to be where "she" has been.

The Mary of the Bible never attracted attention to herself, but always directed others to her son and God, never to herself. At a wedding in Cana she advised the servants of the wedding *"Whatever He says to you, do it."* (John 2:5).

When Mary became pregnant with the Lord Jesus by the Holy Spirit of God, she visited her cousin Elizabeth who was also pregnant. Elizabeth would give birth to John the Baptist the herald of the Messiah. On meeting Mary, Elizabeth cried out

" Blessed are you among women and blessed is the fruit of your womb." (Luke 1:42). Mary replied *"My soul magnifies the Lord and my spirit has rejoiced in God my Saviour. For he has regarded the lowly state of His maidservant. For behold, henceforth all generations will call me blessed. For He who is mighty has done great things for me. And holy is His name....* (Luke 1:46-49)

The Virgin Mary we see portrayed in scripture is a wonderful, humble young woman with a thankful heart toward God. Her reply to Elizabeth is full of praise to the God of Israel. She only mentions herself in passing, in order to praise God for the mercy and love He has shown her in allowing her to be the woman all Jewish women have longed to be. The mother of the Messiah. There is nothing self indulgent about Mary. She continually points us to the mercy of God. This young Jewess serves as an example to all women who would live humbly before their God. The Marian visions of the Roman Catholic Church do exactly the opposite.

True, the apparitions of "Mary" exhort people to pray, to fast, to read the Bible. But the Mary of the apparitions also demands shrines to built in her honour as well as requesting all nations to be dedicated to her

"Immaculate Heart." And this is only scratching the surface. We shall see the Virgin Mary of Roman Catholicism is so far removed from the Mary of the Bible she is now pleading, demanding to be given the tile "Co-Redemptrix" that is, one who saved the world in partnership with Jesus Christ.

Catholic Charismatics trace their origins back to the time in the early 70's when a Catholic student began speaking in tongues whilst reciting the rosary, a medieval string of prayer beads. The Catholic rosary has 50 small beads. Every set of 10 is separated by one larger bead. The 50 beads are for prayers to the Virgin Mary while the 5 larger are for reciting the "Our Father" or "Lord's Prayer." It does not take a mathematician to calculate there are 5 prayers to God and 50 to Mary. But, we are told the Church does not place Mary above or equal to God.

Most of the prayers addressed to Mary on the rosary are the "Hail Mary."

"Hail Mary, full of grace, the Lord is with thee. Blessed art thou among women and blessed is the fruit of thy womb, Jesus. Holy Mary, Mother of God, pray for us sinners now and at the hour of our death."

The rosary usually concludes with the "Hail, Holy Queen."

"Hail, Holy Queen, Mother of Mercy. Hail, our life, our sweetness and our hope. To you do we cry, poor banished children of Eve; to you do we send up our sighs, mourning and weeping, in this valley of tears.

Turn then, most gracious advocate, your eyes of mercy towards us; and after this our exile, show unto us the blessed fruit of your womb, Jesus. O clement, O loving, O sweet Virgin Mary, pray for us, O holy Mother of God. That we may be made worthy of the promises of Christ."

Remember one of the first reported occurrences of a Catholic speaking in tongues was at the time they were reciting one of the above prayers. The supposed message or interpretation of that first message in tongues uttered by a Catholic was to confirm that "Everything our Lady of Fatima said will come true." What "Our Lady of Fatima" said in 1917 was Russia would eventually be converted to Catholicism or rather her "Immaculate Heart" and if we pray the rosary regularly eventually her "Immaculate Heart" will triumph and usher in an age of global peace known to the faithful as the "Marian Age."

This explains, in part, Hitler's endorsement of Catholic missionaries in Russia alongside the Nazi army in the Second World War. The Vatican expected the "prophecy" of "Our Lady of Fatima" to come to pass under the Nazi jackboot. Also the apparition requested that the entire world be dedicated to her "Immaculate heart". Pope John Paul II has now obeyed the vision and dedicated the whole planet to the heart of the Virgin Mary.

The prophesied "Marian age of peace" will very possibly come to pass. But it will not be a gift from God to the planet. Instead it will be a deception satanically foisted upon the world through the fake peace brought about by the rule of Antichrist, with the aid of the false World Religion and the False Prophet, all working in conjunction with one another.

The real Mary of the Bible, the mother of the Lord Jesus, was a wonderful believer. A tremendous example of womanhood, of humble, faithful obedience to God. She is last seen in the Bible in Acts 1 faithfully praying with her fellow disciples awaiting the coming of the Holy Spirit upon the Church at Pentecost. Yet today, I have no doubt, this dear believer would be shocked and dismayed were she to become aware of the cult that surrounds her person. A cult dedicated to diverting the love and adoration of believers away from her son, her Saviour, and toward her. Mary is among the faithful believers who have gone before us into glory. She is alongside those dear Christians of ages past, joining with them in worshipping the Lamb of God. But she is among them, not above them. The Virgin Mary is not, under any circumstances, to have prayers addressed to her. Nowhere in the whole of scripture are we to address our prayers to Mary or to any other saint or angel. God alone is to be prayed to. As a religious Jew of the first century, Mary would be horrified to hear people directing their prayers toward her. But she cannot hear our prayers. She is too busy worshipping her Saviour.

In reality the prayers are being directed to a demonic spirit masquerading as Mary. We shall look at this in a moment. Mary eventually died. To address your prayers to anyone who has died is an abomination to God (Deut. 18:10-12). However, the Roman Catholic

Church gets around this problem by stating Mary, like her son the Lord Jesus, was "assumed bodily into Heaven": "We pronounce, declare and proclaim it to be a Divinely revealed dogma: that the Immaculate Mother of God, the ever Virgin Mary, having completed the course of her earthly life, was assumed body and soul into Heavenly glory." (48)

There is no evidence in the scriptures whatever to support the notion that she was taken bodily into Heaven as the Roman Catholic Church teaches. It is all based on a supposed Divinely inspired authoritative pronouncement from the Pope. What one finds amazing is that this is not some ancient belief made law in the dark ages but one that was pronounced a Divine revelation as recently as 1950!

It was after her "assumption" that Mary was supposedly crowned "Queen over all things" "Queen of Heaven" (49). If this were not bad enough the Catholic Church believes no one obtains salvation without the aid of the Virgin Mary.

"O Virgin most holy, none abounds in the knowledge of God except through thee; none, O mother of God, obtains salvation except through thee, none receives a gift from the throne of mercy except through thee" (50).

The Catholic Church teaches that all gifts from God flow from the Father through Christ who then proceeds to pass them on to the Church through the Virgin Mary. If Mary does not allow those gifts to flow to you from her then you will not receive them. This includes the gift of salvation. Remember the prayer

"...none, O mother of God, obtains salvation except through thee.."

A statement from the much lauded document issued after Vatican II confirms this blasphemous heresy: "God has committed to her (Mary) the treasury of all good things, in order that everyone may know that through her are obtained every hope, every grace, and all salvation. For this is His will that we obtain everything through Mary."(51) Yet we are expected to believe the gift of the Holy Spirit of God is imparted to those who believe and practice such blasphemy!

Moses, in Deuteronomy 13, warns of false leaders who predict events and lead their hearers astray after false gods or goddesses.

1 "If there arises among you a prophet or a dreamer of dreams and he gives you a sign or a wonder,

2 and the sign or the wonder comes to pass, of which he spoke to you saying "Let us go after other gods' -- which you have not known--- and let us serve them."

3 "you shall not listen to the words of that prophet or that dreamer of dreams, for the Lord your God is testing you to know whether you love the Lord your God with all your heart and with all your soul."

Many will say this cannot apply to Mary because she is not a goddess. But that is exactly what she is becoming in the eyes of the Roman Catholic Church as we shall presently prove. I believe it entirely possible that the "peace" promised by the visions will be part of the ultimate last days deception bringing all men and faiths together into a global brotherhood. It is also possible the "apparitions" of the Virgin Mary will be the link between Rome and those of other faiths.

For Buddhists, Liberals, New Agers etc. the idea of a One World Religion bound together by a Mother goddess; channelling messages from higher masters (demons), to a Church headed by their friend the ecumenical Pope of Rome, would not be that big a pill to swallow. Buddhists for instance regard Jesus as an "avatar" an ascended master. Among other faiths Jesus and Mary are highly regarded. For all men to join under one banner would be attractive to many faiths. But what about the religion of Islam with its millions of radical followers around the globe? Would that not pose an insurmountable problem? Not really. Muslims especially venerate the Virgin. The Koran extols Mary.

Also, one of the most revered sites of Marian apparitions is in Fatima, Portugal. The link between this little village and Islam lies in the history of Portugal. Portugal was once ruled by Islam and the village of Fatima was named after one of the daughters of Mohammed. Muslims reason that for Mary to appear in a village named after the prophet's daughter must be a sure sign of her favour toward the Muslim faith and therefore an endorsement of Islam. As Herbert J. Pollitt records in his excellent book "The Inter-Faith Movement" "when a statue of the Virgin Mary was taken through parts of Muslim Africa and Asia, the followers of Islam, Buddhism, Hinduism and Sikhism turned out to venerate the statue and learn of "Our Lady's Peace Plan from Heaven." When the statue reached Mozambique the Muslim Chief of the Ismaeli tribe placed a golden necklace around the statue's neck saying "Thank you, Our Lady of Fatima, for the work you are accomplishing in Africa. We praise you, together with the Almighty Allah." (52)

In 1968 a series of apparitions took place in Egypt above the roof of a Coptic Church in the town of Zeitun. Many thousands of Christians and Muslims gathered to pray to the "apparition of Mary" that was witnessed on television and reported in national newspapers. Below is an alleged photograph taken during a sighting of the apparition in Egypt, which continued on and off for 3 years. Notice the halo of light…the orb of the sun god around the head of the vision. Also the dove above the halo is Babylonian in origin. When Semiramis was deified as "Queen of Heaven" she was also worshiped as Juno the dove. Look at the picture, friends. This is not the mother of the Lord Jesus Christ. This is a demonic spirit complete

with Babylonian regalia. We must be wise in these days. Not accepting everything the spirit world throws at us in the name of God. But we must "test the spirits". Too many today are simply receiving lies from lying and seducing spirits sent forth from the pit in order to lead you astray into the One World Religion emanating from Rome. Beware friends. Beware.

Zeitun is regarded as the place to which Joseph took Mary and the child Jesus when they fled the wrath of King Herod and escaped to Egypt. The Church is built to commemorate that episode in the life of the Messiah. As they flocked to witness the spectacle of the apparition, Muslims prayed from the Koran,

"Mary, God has chosen thee. And purified thee. He has chosen thee above all women."

As well as occurring in most Western nations, such visitations have been increasingly reported in other Islamic countries. The worldwide appeal of the apparitions draws millions from almost every nation. The "cult of the Virgin" has world wide influence. For instance, in Guadalupe in South America, between 15 to 20 million Marian followers, per. year, visit the shrine where Mary is supposed to have appeared in 1531.

In Poland the city of Jasna Gora receives 5 million pilgrims each year to the shrine of the black Madonna. Pope John Paul II has proclaimed her "Queen of Poland."

In Knock, Ireland, millions visit the shrine commemorating the "visitation of the Virgin."

In Lourdes, France, more than 5 and a half million people each year visit the site where, in 1858, a little French girl named Bernadette Soubirous is said to have been visited regularly by the Virgin, a lady in white.

During one of the "Virgin's" visits, Bernadette was commanded by the vision to eat the grass where she was standing. Bernadette did so and we are told a spring of water gushed from the spot. A spring which heals the sick. I am not suggesting sick people have not been healed when visiting the shrine at Lourdes. I cannot say. But those believers who seek God truly may receive a touch from His hand. But because a person is healed is no sign that God is doing the healing. Indeed many Spiritist's and psychics claim to have healing power yet their belief that they are in touch with spirit beings is strictly condemned in scripture. If this is so then why Christianise the story of a shrine where a lady appears from the other world and purports to give healing power to that particular area? Simply because she claims to be Mary is no proof. In fact that is the very evidence for believing the vision is not of God. Nowhere in scripture are we told to have contact with the spirits of those who have gone on before. In fact it is soundly anti-scriptural.

"Give no regard to mediums and familiar spirits; do not seek after them, to be defiled by them: I am the Lord your God"
Lev. 19:31.

Also Deuteronomy 18:10-12 *"There shall not be found among you anyone who makes his son or daughter pass through the fire, or one who practices witchcraft, or a soothsayer, or one who interprets omens, or a sorcerer, or one who conjures spells, or a medium, or a spiritist, or one who calls up the dead. For all these things are an abomination to the Lord......"*

But the Catholic Church in claiming to have contact with Mary and various dead "saints" is guilty of attempting to communicate with the dead. In fact there is ample evidence from the mouths of these "visions" that what is taking place is not something good. But something very deceptive and dark.

As an aside, Catholic monk Padre Pio was a man who claimed to have the marks of Christ's passion on his body. His hands, feet and side were said to bleed regularly. Pio believed his suffering helped gain early release to those who had died and gone to purgatory. He claimed that through his suffering many souls were released from purgatory because he had helped to pay for their sins. Total blasphemy one may say. The book of Hebrews states clearly "Christ died for our sins once and for all." In other words there is nothing more that can be done to save me. Christ and Christ alone did it all. Yet it is said voices were heard coming from Pio's cell at night as countless numbers of the redeemed stopped by to thank him as they made their way from purgatory to Heaven. I believe this deceived man was visited by evil spirits claiming to be believers on their way to Heaven thanks to him. Pio has now been made a saint by the Catholic Church. One to whom many pray for help. And this is the religion to which so many Protestants want to return.

All around the globe the apparitions of a woman in bright clothing claiming to be the Virgin Mary are on the increase. It has been estimated there were more apparitions of "Mary" in the 20th century than in the 300 years that went before.

What does the Pope think about these apparitions and about Mary herself? John Paul II has visited as many apparition sites around the world as he can. As he does so he tirelessly campaigns for greater understanding between the worlds faiths. As was stated earlier, he has dedicated his entire Pontificate to the Virgin Mary. Not to the Lord Jesus Christ. Surely that act alone should sound alarm bells in the ears of any Bible believer. He is known in Catholic circles as "Mary's Pope."

In the book "Crossing the Threshold of Hope" John Paul II writes

"If victory comes it will be brought about by Mary. Christ will conquer through her. Because he wants the Church's victories now and in the future to be linked to her." (53)

May I ask a simple question? How does he know? Who told him this? Did he read this in the Bible? No. Such a belief is nowhere to be found in the scriptures. It is simply the product of his wishful and imaginative thinking. Yet no one dares ask, even though it is obvious the "emperor" has no clothes.

So many who call themselves Christians believe the apparitions could indeed be the Virgin Mary. "Why not?" they ask. The Bible must be our only guide regarding all matters. That includes apparitions and messages from the "spirit world". What does it have to say? What do the apparitions say? Paul the apostle, who was used to visions and Heavenly instruction, warned his readers:

"But even if we or an angel from Heaven preach any other Gospel to you than what we have preached to you let him be accursed."
Gal. 1:8

He also warned of the deceptiveness of Satan

" And no wonder! For Satan himself transforms himself into an angel of light."
2 Cor. 11:14

Do the apparitions of Mary preach a different Gospel to the one Paul preached? Is the Mary of the visionaries in reality a messenger of Satan? A demonic entity masquerading as the mother of our Lord Jesus Christ? If so what is the purpose behind the visions? Let us compare the statements of the "visions" with the clear word of God. We do this, not with an air of superiority but with one of deep concern for all who truly wish to follow and know God and the Lord Jesus. When compared with one another the statements made by the apparitions and the statements found in the Bible are totally contradictory. But the claims and statements made by the Catholic "Mary" do give us a clue as to the goals and the agenda of the spiritual forces behind the visions. What is discovered is something highly dangerous and incredibly deceptive.

"I am the Mediatrix (mediator) between you and God."
Vision at Medjugorja, Yugoslavia

"For there is one God and one meiator between God and men, the man Christ Jesus."
1 Timothy 2:5

That one bible verse reveals the "Mary" of the visions to be different to the Mary of the Bible. The Bible tells us plainly our dear Lord Jesus, Himself, is the only mediator.

"The world is degenerating. So much so that it was necessary for the Father and the Son to send me into the world. Among all the peoples in order to be their Advocate and to save them."
Vision of "Our Lady of all Nations, Holland

"If any man sins we have an Advocate with the Father, Jesus Christ the righteous."
1 John 2:1

Again, Christ alone is our advocate as well as our mediator, not Mary.

"I call upon you to open yourselves completely to me. So that through each of you I may be enabled to convert and save the world."
Vision at Medjugorja, Yugoslavia

"I alone am able still to save you from the calamities which approach. Those who place their confidence in me will be saved."
Vision of our Lady of Akita (Japan)

In this time I am the ark for all your brethren. I am the ark of peace. I am the ark of salvation. The ark where my children must enter if they wish to live in the Kingdom of God."
Vision of Our Lady of San Nicolas

"For God did not send His Son into the world to condemn the world, but that the world through Him might be saved."
John 3:16

"Look to me and be saved, All you ends of the earth! For I am God and there is no other."
Isa.45:22

Peter speaking of Jesus… *"Nor is there salvation in any other name under Heaven given among men by which we must be saved."*
Acts 4:12

Need we say more? But the visions continue…

"Do not be grieved. I am with all of you even though you do not see me. I am mother of all of you sinners."
Message given in Nicaragua

"Lo I am with you always, even to the end of the age"
Jesus in Matthew 28:20

"I stand here as the co-redemptrix and Advocate. Everything should be concentrated on that. Repeat this after me. The new dogma will be the dogma of the co-redemptrix."
Vision of The Lady of All Nations. (Holland)

"Until I am acknowledged there, where the most Holy Trinity has willed me to be, I will not be able to exercise my power fully. In the maternal work of co-redemption and of the universal mediation of graces."
<u>Message given to Father Gobbi</u>

"For a long time I have suffered for you. If I do not want my son to abandon you I am forced to pray to Him myself without ceasing …..(Y)ou can never recompense the pain I have taken for you."
<u>Vision of Our Lady of LaSalette, France</u>

" …*I, the Lord am your Saviour, And your Redeemer, the Mighty One of Jacob.*"
<u>Isa. 45:26b</u>

"In Him we have redemption through His blood, the forgiveness of sins, according to the riches of His grace."
<u>Eph. 1:7</u>

.You have redeemed us to God by your blood…"
<u>Rev. 5:9</u>

For an excellent video, "Messages From Heaven" documenting the visions please contact National Prayer Network. London. England.

Not once in the entire Bible, in prophetic utterances or as related by Jesus Christ or the Apostles, is Mary portrayed as possessing any of the titles or powers accorded to the Mary of the visions. On such evidence one is forced to conclude the visions of Mary are not visitations of the real mother of our Lord. But that they are deceptions. I believe they are part of a spiritual deception coming upon the earth in these last days. A deception designed to draw believers away from the truth of the Bible and to cause them to give heed to "seducing spirits" as the scripture warns in 1Tim. 4:1-3 and 2 Tim. 3:1-9 among others.

The Mary of Catholicism is a pagan goddess.

Some may balk at such an assertion but when the visions claim to be advocate, mediator, saviour, co-redeemer, present with all believers and so much more, we are speaking of a goddess not a human being. No one other than a divine personage could claim to be with believers everywhere which is what the visions claim. To be everywhere present at the same time is omnipresence. An attribute of Deity.

Non can lay claim to be able to save the world apart from a divine person. From Genesis to Malachi the Old Testament speaks of a coming one, the Messiah who would suffer for the sins of the world. The New Testament from Matthew to Revelation reveals this one to be Jesus Christ. Yet not once is there any reference suggesting the Messiah would or did suffer as part of a team effort along with His mother or any one else for that matter. Not one word mentions Mary as redeeming the world with her son. Yet that is what the visions would have us accept. And it is what the visions have managed to have the Catholic Church and its adherents receive gladly. In fact many believe the next major Church dogma will be to grant Mary the official title of Co-redemptrix. This is what the apostles would call a false Gospel. A Gospel which presents a false salvation.

To trust in any one for your salvation, other than Jesus Christ alone, is to believe a false Gospel and hence a false salvation. If you do so you remain lost in your sins and on your way to Hell. What a terrifying thought this is to consider. Dear friends may we urge you in love, place your trust in Christ and Him alone and you shall be saved. Do not trust the unscriptural teachings of Rome and the claims of demonic apparitions. These are mere ploys of the enemy to draw souls from around the world into the arms of Rome and Satan's last days religion in which sinful man will be deified.

Many Christians, in these last days, are woefully ignorant of scriptural truth and of Catholic heresy. They are blissfully unaware of the catastrophic trap into which they are merrily leading their Churches.

Mark this, the coming union many will enter into with Rome will be on Rome's terms. Her motto is semper eadem, always the same. She will never change.

Many may ask "Don't we all believe the same now?"

"Didn't Vatican II in the 1960's change most of our differences?" No, it did not.

In fact we have shown earlier in this book, Vatican II upheld the teachings of the council of Trent, which state in clear and unmistakable terms that to believe a man can be saved by faith in Christ alone means you are cursed. That is a fact of history and the official teaching of the Roman Catholic Church. Not one major dogma of the council of Trent was changed by Vatican II. Ecumenism unbridled will ultimately outlaw the truth which states Jesus Christ is the only yourselves with Church unity activities will one day wake up to discover, all too late, the Gospel your forefathers lived and died to promote has been done away with. And the Almighty will hold you responsible for having been too weak to stand and be counted when you were needed. Maybe in your sincerity to see all Christians come together you have overlooked the errors of Rome. But you are in error yourself and some would accuse you of being too afraid to face the truth. Your silence at this time will allow the enemy of our souls to hand out, nquestioned, unhindered, a false salvation offered way to Heaven. Remember, you who involve by a false religion from Rome.

You will have helped trusting souls, who looked to you for guidance, to enter the wide door which leads to the Church of Babylon, the worship of the Mother Goddess, her false Jesus and ultimately the very flames of Hell. Beware of the road you are taking. You are walking a very dangerous path.

You are on a collision course with the Almighty.

This author believes there is coming a period of unprecedented lawlessness and terror for the world. When this time comes upon us I believe it possible the Mary of the Roman Catholic Church will appear more regularly and in more countries urging men of all faiths to join together under one spiritual ruler, the Pope of Rome. She will also urge all governments to lay down their age old notions of national sovereignty and in their place take up the banner of a united world under one political head, the coming Antichrist. As we shall see in the next chapter the Vatican is not a benign spiritual organism but is deeply involved in world politics. An activity she agreed never to be involved with when she signed the Lateran treaty.

Chapter 11

THE VATICAN AND THE POLITICS OF THE NEW WORLD ORDER

I find it very difficult not to believe we are living in the days of the ten toes of Nebuchadnezzar's image. These are the days when the woman of Revelation 17 is making many professing Christians drunk with the wine of her fornication and enticing them into her bed. Days when she is also preparing to ride the ascending European Roman Empire. What influence, if any, does the Roman Catholic Church have within the present European Union?

As was stated earlier, for centuries the dream of the Roman Catholic Church has been to return to the glory days of Rome. Today thanks to the betrayal of biblical truth by those employed and ordained to protect and uphold it and by lying politicians who constantly assure us our sovereignty is not at stake when all around we see it vanishing, Rome and the faceless unelected bureaucrats in Brussels and Strasbourg are on the verge of realising the fulfilment of that demonically inspired dream.

Today history is repeating itself in Europe. For many years the powerful Western nations have sought for ways to slice Yugoslavia into pieces in order to make the area weaker and easier to control. The war in the Balkans between Bosnia, Serbia and Croatia, was not instigated by the Serbs although the resulting Serbian atrocities, if proved, were indefensible.

The Serbian action was in response to a threat that has been a thorn in their side for years. A threat to divide Yugoslavia and offer her, on the altar of a United (Catholic) Europe, as we noted earlier when we looked at World War II. As the 1980's drew to a close it was said Croatia was receiving arms shipments purportedly financed by her Second World War ally, the Vatican. Some shipments were costing as much as $3 million per deal. At the same time, President Alija Izetbegovic was on the verge of declaring Bosnia an independent Islamic state. To the Serb population of Bosnia this was a terrifying prospect. Predominantly Islamic Bosnia is supported, and financed, by Iran. In 1992 Iran sent $10 million in "humanitarian aid" to Bosnia and later hundreds of Iranian "Revolutionary Guards."

Bosnian President Izetgovic stated "There can be no peace or coexistence between Islamic faith and non-Islamic faith and institutions... The Islamic movement must and can take power as soon as it is morally and numerically strong enough, not only to destroy the non-Islamic power, but to build up a new Islamic one...: (54).

Croatian President Tudjman wrote "Genocide is a natural phenomenon, in harmony with the societal and mythologically divine nature. Genocide is not only permitted, it is also recommended, even commanded by the word of the Almighty, whenever it is useful for the survival or the restoration of the kingdom of the chosen nation, or for the preservation and spreading of its one and only correct faith"(55). Presumably the Catholic faith.

During the resulting conflict between Islamic Bosnia, Orthodox Christian Serbia and Catholic Croatia, Afghanistan sent hundreds of men to fight the "Jihad" for Bosnia. The allies said nothing. The war and the resulting violence and suffering has resulted in far more Serbian refugees than Croatian or Bosnian combined. Today reported Croatian, Bosnian and NATO atrocities against Serbs, and each other, are virtually ignored while those reportedly committed by the Serbs are highlighted.

Following the outbreak of war in the Balkans in the early 1990's and the subsequent cease-fire, strict curbs were put in place by the allies to prevent an arms build up in the region between Croatia, Bosnia and Serbia. However the Vatican managed to circumvent these curbs through behind the scenes moves in America's halls of power. Subsequently after Croatia's peace pact with Bosnia, aided by America (and some say Vatican finances) Croatia was able to rearm itself and attack Serbia which at this point was seriously weak and possessed very few arms.

The Croatian military were even accorded State Department passes enabling them to visit U.S. bases for special courses. However, the allies had ensured the arms embargo against Serbia had, all the while, stayed in place. In the meantime the American State Department co-ordinated an attempt to assist the Catholic Croatian and Islamic Bosnian forces to work together. Croatia also received advanced American computer technology and fire control system technology to enable the Croats to gain the upper hand on the battlefield (56).

Serbia was bombed into defeat by the "victorious" NATO forces who reportedly used bombs and missiles containing depleted uranium. In other words the allies waged a "low intensity nuclear war" against the civilian Serbian population. But we are assured this was not a war crime. This was a successful "humanitarian action" conducted in an effort to rescue the area from the ethnic cleansing reportedly being conducted by Milosovic. But as has been noted earlier, it is the alleged Serbian atrocities that are remembered while atrocities said to have been committed by Bosnians, Croatians and their allies are conveniently ignored by the majority of the worlds media. Even though the West promised to rebuild Serbia much of the country remains in ruins.

Today former Serbian President Slobodan Milosevic is standing trial for war crimes. It is not our place to say whether or not he is guilty of the charges. But it is interesting to note at present no other leader is being arrested for crimes against humanity despite reports of atrocities being committed by all sides in the Balkans including NATO. There are reports by Muslims against their own people. Among the accusations are reports of Serbian civilians being beheaded by Croats and Muslims, the heads then being kicked around the streets. Muslims are heavily suspected of exploding a device in a Bosnian market killing many of their own Muslim people. However while the evidence pointed to the Muslims it was the Serbs who were instantly accused of the crime.

In the drive for a unified Europe with a Catholic Church holding the spiritual reins, a leader, as strong as Milosevic (regardless of his faults or redeeming qualities) in charge of a united Yugoslavia was unthinkable. He had to go. A fragmented, weakened and defeated Yugoslavia could be controlled by the men of the New World Order and the European empire. Interestingly at the time of the Balkans conflict U.S. congressman Lantos stated "At the end of the day, and it may be a few years down the road, neither Serbia nor Croatia nor Macedonia nor Kosovo will be able to function unless they are part of a United Europe." How insightful.

A strong, united Yugoslavia led by Milosevic, good or bad, could not be so easily manipulated by the rising empire. But it seems an Islamic Bosnia, supported by Iran which also supports terrorist groups such as Hamas, Hizb'allah and Islamic Jihad, is, for the moment, acceptable. And a Catholic Croatia is also less challenging. In fact Islam, as we have seen, is a tentative friend of Catholicism and the Vatican. And we must not upset the Vatican's friends or her plans for Europe, the Middle East and the rest of the world must we? At least not until things are comfortably in place.

In Great Britain Margaret Thatcher was, in some ways, an ardent anti-Europhile. But the European empire and its disciples drew out their knives and in no time she was gone. You cannot have a leader who is determined to hang on to national sovereignty. Not in this new world.

As we look around the globe there are dictators and

bullies who have been left to continue their reign of terror and misery. They are not too much of a problem. They do not live in Europe. But as Europe settles into her new shoes as Empress of the West their days will be numbered as the N.W.O. spreads its tentacles across an ever darkening world, rooting out all dissenters. Good or evil.

Iraqi President Saddam Hussein is still free. Even though he is believed to have had thousands of his own people murdered. Saddam was given the wherewithal to create biological and chemical weapons in shipments supplied by the West notably America to aid him in his 10 year war against Iran.

Iran had humiliated the U.S.A. back in the late 1970's when the Islamic revolution unceremoniously and in front of the world's media expelled most Americans and held some as hostages in the American Embassy in Tehran. The USA attempted a rescue of the hostages.

This "secret" mission was a disaster from the very beginning when two U.S. helicopters, on their way to perform the rescue, mistakenly landed by the side of a busy Iranian motorway where they were seen by incredulous Iraqi civilians travelling past in cars and buses. In a desperate attempt to get back into the air the two helicopters took off and collided with each other killing all on board. Following this embarrassing debacle and presumably, rather than go to war with Iran (which has now tentatively become a friend of the Vatican) and risk the possibility of an Islamic backlash against them, which they have now received anyway, the Americans supplied Saddam with the biological and chemical means to wage war against Iran. Now Saddam, too, has outlived his usefulness and may be removed at last. Although he, like Bush and other leaders, is a top Freemason and it may be difficult to oust a brother of the Secret Order. Also Saddam is secretly threatening to unleash smallpox on the world if he is attacked by the West. We must wait and see if his threat is real or false. Could the truth surrounding the West's hatred of Saddam Hussein have something to do with the fact that American oil production peaked in the 1970's and has been in decline ever since? It is expected to run out completely around the year 2030.

Yet more and more consumers are demanding oil to perpetuate their standard of living. America desperately needs to discover a new source. Yet all recent oil explorations have proved to be of little value.

Where will America and her Western allies go? Iraq is run by a tyrant we all agree. And Iraq produces 10% of the world's oil!

Behind the scenes future Western control of Iraq and the rebuilt city of Babylon could play an enormously prophetic part in the coming days (Rev. 18).

Iran, in the meantime, is on the verge of developing its own nuclear weapons. Yet, for the moment, it too is left unchallenged. But not for long. The N.W.O. will ensure any other nation, threatening their plans for you and I are quickly brought to heel.
Where is the leader of the al-Qaeda terrorist organisation, Osama Bin Laden who had his base in Afghanistan and from there supposedly organised the

despicable acts of September 11th? No one seems to know. But it is suspected that many of his followers escaped Afghanistan and are now "sleeping" in the West.

Around 100 suitcase sized nuclear devices vanished from the former USSR during the 1990's. It is feared some may be in the hands of Islamic "sleepers" awaiting their call to awake and detonate their weapons, *whatever they may be*, in a Western city.

While considering Afghanistan it is interesting to contemplate the report that American intelligence briefed Pakistani and Russian intelligence agencies of America's intention to attack Afghanistan two months *before* the attack on the World Trade Centre caused the world to look on that country as a centre for terrorism(57). Why? Well, apart from housing terrorists and repressing its own people, the ruling Taliban were also blocking the opening of a lucrative oil pipeline to the West. Once again oil not freedom would appear to be a major factor in ousting regimes not falling in line with the New World Order. Needless to say, now the West has driven the Taliban into the hills and brought in a government more sympathetic to the West, the oil pipeline is back on the table.

September 11th merely gave the West the excuse they needed. Many believe terrorist Bin Laden is a useful tool in the hands of the N.W.O. in that he is the bogey man who could cause people to call for a World Government to protect them. Why kill him (yet)? He is of more use to the N.W.O. alive than dead. But when his usefulness runs out the West will need to dispose of him or invent a new "threat to the Western World and the Middle East." Palestinian leader Yasser Arafat is the head of the terrorist organisation the PLO. Under his leadership these terrorists have murdered many, many innocents. Jewish, Palestinian and Arab. Yet Arafat has never been brought to book for his crimes. In spite of the fact that when he was in Jordan he waged war against King Hussein, killing many hundreds of civilians and breaking 22 cease fire agreements along the way. Hussein eventually forced Arafat and the PLO out and they headed for Lebanon where they murdered Christians, destroyed Christian towns and villages, decimated the country and continually fired shells and sent killers across the border into northern Israel. When they were eventually thrown out of Lebanon by the Israeli's they left behind more than 300,000 dead civilians and 100,000 pregnant young women. Incredibly, when leaving Lebanon, Arafat and the PLO were protected by the United Nations. Since settling in the West Bank as the voice of the Palestinian people, Arafat, the PLO and the terrorist groups they shake hands with such as Hizb'allah, Islamic Jihad and Hamas have persistently seen to it that cease fires with Israel are broken in a bloodbath of suicide bombings and shootings, claiming the lives of many innocent Israeli's. Yet when Israel retaliates and pursues the guilty parties after months of carnage unleashed on their people, the world holds its hands up in horror.

One thing the Western democracies seem to miss is the fact that the Middle East problem is not political. It is religious. It is spiritual. Tremendous unseen forces are at work in this corner of the world. For centuries the land now known as Israel was under Islam though it was never a recognised state. Palestine was a desert place. But according to the teachings of Islam any land that was once Islamic and is now ruled over by another faith must be regained for Allah. The avowed intention is not peace with Israel but her annihilation.

The same goes for Europe. Much of Europe was under Muslim rule until the Middle Ages. Many Muslims believe Europe must be re-islamicised. Today in Britain mosques are being erected almost weekly as more and more Westerners turn to Islam.

I believe it entirely possible in the coming days Islam, the Roman Catholic Church and the World Government will, together, relegate true Christianity into an outdated relic of a bygone age.

In the Middle East any Palestinian who is suspected of aiding Israel risks being beaten to death or shot and hung up by the heels, as happened twice recently in Bethlehem. An event the majority of the world press ignored. It is well known by most governments that Arafat recently spoke of a Middle East peace to Western journalists. Afterwards he went on Arabic radio calling for suicide bombers. The PLO has stated "It is not Israel's borders that are the problem, but Israel's existence."

How has the world treated Arafat, who reportedly committed his first murder when he was 20? He has become a friend of the Pope. Arafat has been a regular visitor to the Vatican since the 1960's. The Vatican makes overtures to Israel while denying her right to her ancient capital, Jerusalem. The Catholic Church refers to the Jews as the "..people *formerly* called the people of

God." According to Catholic theology that title has now passed to the Catholic Church. In spite of the many scriptures yet to be fulfilled concerning Israel and the Jewish people many "Christians" believe the Jews are finished as far as the promises of God are concerned. "All the unfulfilled promises will be fulfilled in the church not Israel" they say. If that is so and God can make promises to a people today and give them to another tomorrow how can we trust He will not give them to someone else other than the church in the future?

His promises are not recalled. All the promises to the Jewish people will yet come to pass literally before our eyes.

God does not lie.

The Vatican insists Jerusalem should belong to the Palestinians or at worst be an international city. Her true sympathies appear to lie with her friends in the PLO. When Pope John Paul II visited the Middle East in 2000 Arafat welcomed him into Bethlehem to celebrate "our Jesus Christ, the Palestinian freedom fighter." The aged Pope smiled at his friend and accepted the welcome. To add to the sickening cycle of hypocrisy the world handed Arafat the Nobel Peace Prize. It would seem as long the shadowy men of the New World Order see something in you they can use to further their globalist agenda, you are safe. When you are no longer of any use you become a threat to world peace. Arafat may soon go, since he rejected the Israeli offer of 97% of his demands at camp David in 2000.

Many believe the decision to force Israel to make such a generous offer was agreed upon at the secret Bilderberg meeting held in Portugal in 1999 even though no Israeli leader was invited. But Arafat and the Pope were invited. At that time Arafat agreed to accept the plan. His New World Order masters were displeased to say the least when Arafat later turned it down. Now his masters or ill health may soon see him removed to make way for a World Government puppet. But the Pope will surely have some say about the man who will fill the shoes of his friend Yasser Arafat.

Back in Europe the Vatican dream of a United Catholic Europe marches on virtually unhindered as Catholic politicians manoeuvre for ever closer union. The Vatican has overseen the re-dividing of Czechoslovakia and the separating of Catholic Slovakia. Switzerland, the land of Zwingli and Calvin, will, very soon be surrounded by Catholic nations.

The former Soviet Union has disintegrated into small states, some of which, including the Ukraine, have large Roman Catholic populations.

Pope John Paul II's homeland, Poland has been re-Romanised through the co-operation between the Vatican and the Solidarnosc Movement. The Vatican is said to have contributed millions of dollars to assist Solidarnosc in its battle to overthrow the Communist government and set up a "Catholic" government in its place. A recent Italian film suggests the Vatican used laundered Mafia money to fund Solidarnosc. Solidarnosc's leader, Lec Walesa, an ardent Roman

Catholic, subsequently became President. Shortly after his election, Walesa entered the Vatican and declared to Pope John Paul II " I offer you our new Poland" (58).

When the Soviet Union collapsed, many intelligence agencies in the West were surprised by the suddenness of events.

The Vatican was not.

Over the years it had supplied huge amounts in finance to assist anti-Communist activities in Eastern Europe. In fact as the U.S.S.R. fell the Vatican advised Western governments "Listen to the Holy Father. We have 2,000 years experience in this kind of thing."

Concerning the fall of the Soviet Union and its satellites Mikhail Gorbachev wrote "One can say that everything that has happened in Eastern Europe in recent years would have been impossible without the Pope's efforts and the enormous role, including the political role, he has played in the world's arena" (59).

Also, many mistakenly believe Mikhail Gorbachev has vanished from the world political scene and is now a spent force. Nothing could be further from the truth. In 1992 he set up the "Gorbachev Foundation". There is a branch in Moscow. Another is to be found in San Francisco at the "Presidio" a former U.S. military base. Does that not amaze you? The former head of the U.S.S.R. now having his headquarters in America in a former military base? The Gorbachev foundation is his vehicle to promote the concept of World Government. Former President Gorbachev travels the world as an evangelist for the New World Order.

Every autumn, beginning in 1995, Mikhail Gorbachev chairs the "State of the World Forum.." The people he invites to these conferences read like a "who's who" of the world's politicians, religious leaders, New Age gurus and Occultists. This is all run in unison with the European Union and the United Nations as they seek to bring about a New World Order and New World Religion.

Among those included on the Board of Directors of the Gorbachev Foundation is Father Theodore Hesbrook former President of Notre Dame University and one of the Catholic Church's foremost educators.

In June 2000 a new ecumenical organisation was formed. Named "THE UNITED RELIGIONS" it has been given its headquarters in the "Presidio" the exact same place where we find the headquarters of the Gorbachev Foundation. Religious leaders from all faiths are promoting this evil mockery of true faith in God. I believe this will eventually be linked with the coming false World Religion based in Rome. But what is the link between Gorbachev and Rome?

On December 1st 1989 Mikhail Gorbachev, former leader of Communist U.S.S.R. entered the Vatican. He knelt before Pope John Paul II and begged forgiveness of all his sins. He later said "What I have always held in high esteem about the Pope's thinking and ideas is their spiritual content and their striving to foster the development of a New World Civilisation." It is clear to see that Gorbachev regards the Pope as a spiritual and political "comrade" joining him on his quest for a New World Order.

The Vatican has ears everywhere. It has 116 embassies around the globe. With its emissaries, institutions and priests it is in a unique position to help and influence this demonically inspired anti God World Government when it appears.

Former Jesuit and Vatican insider, Malachi Martin, believes the Vatican would not even have to change gear to accommodate the new empire. He writes "What captures the unwavering attention of the secular leaders of the world in this remarkable network of the Roman Catholic Church is precisely the fact that it places at the personal disposal of the Pope a supranational, supercontinental, supra-trade-bloc structure that is so built and orientated that if tomorrow or next week, by a sudden miracle, a One-World Government were established, the Church would not have to undergo any essential change in order to retain its dominant position and to further its global aims" (60).

The Vatican plan for Europe and beyond continues to gain ground while the watch dogs of democracy sleep.

It also would appear the Vatican involvement in politics is not confined to the European continent but its tentacles reach around the globe.

Roberto Calvi was Chairman of Italy's largest private bank, Banco Ambrosiano. The bank had close links with the Vatican bank, The Institute for Religious Affairs. Also, Calvi was a member of the ultra shady, right wing Masonic group known as P2. It is well known that many in the hierarchy of the Catholic Church are suspected of being members of P2. It is believed the present Pope's predecessor, Pope John Paul I, was in the process of drawing up plans to demote and remove to less powerful positions, those members of the Catholic hierarchy who were involved with P2. Unfortunately he died under very mysterious circumstances just as he was about to bring his plans down upon the heads of those concerned. One may assume Calvi would have been quite aware of the Catholic Church's involvement with the powerful men inside P2. So close was his association with the Vatican, Calvi was given the nickname "God's banker." This man had, apparently, become deeply involved in Vatican operations. According to a letter Calvi wrote to an unknown addressee, he had "provided financing throughout Latin America for warships and other military equipment to be used to counter the subversive activities of well organised Communist forces." Calvi claimed to have also provided $175 million for the establishment of "financial centres and political power to 5 Latin American countries."

He states earlier in the same letter he had done this "on behalf of the representatives of St. Peter."

Around the time of writing this letter, demanding reimbursement for his services, the Banco Ambrosiano collapsed with huge debts when it was revealed the bank was being used to launder Mafia money. Many believed the trail also led to the Vatican bank. Calvi was said to have constantly carried a bulging briefcase which he never let out of his sight. It has been said it contained papers, which, if released, would blow the lid off the Vatican.

In 1983 shortly after writing the above letter Roberto Calvi was discovered hanging by his neck from scaffolding beneath Blackfriars Bridge, London. His pockets were stuffed with bricks.
Whether it was suicide or murder has never been satisfactorily proved. But a recent forensic investigation of the events surrounding Calvi's death point more toward murder. If it was murder most commentators believe it was a Mafia hit. A punishment for mishandling Mafia money.

After Calvi's death the not so bulging briefcase was opened. It was empty. Did Roberto Calvi step on the toes of the powerful men of the Mafia, or those connected with P2 inside the Vatican who feared he may open his mouth to reveal the depth of freemasonry involvement within the Church? More recent evidence suggests Calvi was murdered to prevent him revealing details of links between P2, the Mafia and the Vatican. Someone knows, somewhere.

But they are not saying anything. It is a painful truth that the world is permitted to receive only what the powerbrokers behind the scenes feel we need to know. The flow of information in some areas has never been so clandestine and selective. Very often what we are fed is not the truth, as has been witnessed in Israel and her war against terrorism where downright biased reporting and falsehoods abound to the detriment of the Israelis.
This Satanically inspired anti-Semitism against Israel will grow globally until it very possibly results in an

international presence in Israel and the West Bank. A move desired for many years by the Western nations and the Vatican wishing to gain a foothold in the ancient land bridge between Asia and Europe. When this happens, who among the radical side of Islam will not suspect the West of casting an eye eastward toward the lucrative oil fields of the Gulf States. All this could lead on, in just a few short years, to the fulfilment of Ezekiel 38, 39 which predict an invasion of the Middle East by forces from the north of Israel. Thought by different scholars to be Russia or Turkey. It will be an invasion resulting in an ignominious end on the mountains of Israel when the God of the Jews arises to defend her. How He will accomplish this defeat of Israel's enemies is not for us to say. It could be supernatural in origin or a defensive move by Israel herself or by the Western nations who have a vested interest in that region. God uses the means he pleases to fulfil his purposes, and make no mistake about it, God has determined that Israel will not be destroyed.

Further, this could lead on to the fulfilment of Zechariah 14 when all nations (the U.N./E.U. World Government?), including the Antichrist himself, come against Jerusalem. This final attack against the Jewish capital by the Gentile nations will be the keg of dynamite that brings about the physical return to Earth of the Lord Jesus to rescue His ancient people and set up His kingdom in Jerusalem for 1,000 years. Only then will peace finally descend upon this troubled region as the King of Kings brings reconciliation between Jew and Arab, uniting Egypt, Israel and Assyria not only spiritually but physically with a highway connecting the three (Isa. 19). But interesting though this is, it is still future and not strictly part of this study. All we may say at present is two things.

Watch for the man who makes peace between Israel and her neighbours. According to the ancient prophecies the man who makes peace in the Middle East could be the Antichrist. And if you are against Israel's right to her land, take care. You are marching out of step with God and His plans for the only area on planet Earth He declares to be His land.

Since the re-birth of Israel no one has achieved peace between these warring cousins. But one man will achieve the seemingly impossible. And strange as it seems he will be the man of whom we must beware. Watch that man. It will be he who will bring such misery upon the globe with his iron fisted, anti-God, rule. It is evident to all with ears to hear and eyes to see, the current international moves are leading inexorably toward a One World Government with a One World Religion at its side based in Rome, Jerusalem and possibly the rebuilt city of Babylon in Iraq. Which makes the current plans of the West to depose Saddam Hussein all the more interesting.

Will the masters of the New World Order set up a centre of activity and commerce in and around the ancient city of Babylon? Many students of Bible prophecy believe the ancient city will still play a future role in the last days. They believe the name Babylon is a term used for Rome, the false religious system and the actual city of Babylon recently rebuilt by Saddam Hussein. We must wait and see. It would appear many prophecies concerning the destruction of the city of

Babylon were not completely fulfilled when she fell under Cyrus but they wait a yet future day. Many Christians have, for centuries, believed this point indicates the future rebuilding of the city of Babylon. An event unseen until today when so many other end time prophecies are appearing before our eyes.

The movers and shakers behind the scenes of world events are very powerful and very determined to birth the New Order. Woes betide you if you stand in their way. These men are ruthless and do not have time for the niceties of civilised negotiation. They mean business. They have an enormous amount of international money and power behind them. They will not be put off easily. They will not be put off at all! Although the coming government will be headed by the man the Bible calls "the beast" and "Antichrist" and the religion will be headed by the man the Bible calls the "second beast" and "false prophet" (Rev. 13: 1-18; 19: 19-21), the world in general will welcome this world leader and his "prophet."

It is amazing that for the last 3,000 years the warnings of the Hebrew prophets relating to the days immediately prior to the return of Jesus Christ have been available for us to read. Equally amazing is the fact that so many refuse to heed these warnings. Instead the majority on planet earth will accept the very men scripture so clearly warns will appear in these days. Two demonically inspired men who will lead the world in a rebellion against God Himself. A rebellion which will lead you to the very pit of Hell should you support them in their evil, yet mercifully short, careers. I believe the World Government and World Religion will rise from the flames of a coming crisis. It will either originate from outside the New World Order group or it will be contrived by them. Either way the men who wish to see a World Government in place will use the coming crisis to make their plans more palatable to a world desperate for stability and leadership.

As the political leader, Antichrist, steps into the limelight to take over the reins of World Government, who do you think he will he promote alongside himself to birth a new spiritual age, calling all faiths to pull together in this time of crisis? I believe it will be the Pope of Rome. Others have said they feel it will be a religious Israeli leader. But I do not think that scenario fits all the scriptures concerning his rise and demise. The Arabs are more lightly to listen to the Pope than to an Israeli.

In the book "The Mind of John Paul II" by George H. Williams, written in praise of the Pope, we read how he was confronted with a dangerous situation during World War II: "How he conducted himself in a tense situation in his native Cracow two score years ago may be prophetic of how in some tense situation for our planetary city in a coming score of years he may with comparable steadiness of nerve deliver a saving word for all mankind."

The present Pope may fail through age to lead the world into the full awfulness of the Whore of Babylon. But another will follow on his heels. One who will be satanically endued with power for such a despicable task. And when this coming world crisis so full of prophetic import occurs, the Vatican will be ready to ride and guide the "New World Order" into a false utopian age of world brotherhood and deceptive spirituality. Then, just like the fabled Pied Piper, she will lead many blind, uninformed souls away from the light and into an infernal darkness from which many will never return. He will draw them back into a Europe that has not been seen since before the Reformation. But a Europe where Rome reigns as Queen over a melting pot of faiths.

A darkened Europe where the true Gospel light will be snuffed out and true Evangelical Christians will be viewed as divisive, bigoted and worthy of imprisonment. Then Rome will begin her reign as Queen, not only in Europe but across the planet. Her diabolical net will spread and tighten like some infernal, incurable cancer from which there will seem to be no escape. As the kingdom of the Antichrist arises from within the European Union, the Vatican, friend of Nazis, terrorists and every false religion under the sun, will be ready.

How close we are to such a monstrosity being birthed we cannot say. But already within the United Nations and other organisations we are able to discern plans being laid for just such an event. Also within the present European Union we are able to see the signs of Vatican involvement and apocalyptic symbolism mirroring the book of Revelation. They are clear to any discerning eye.

Let us now look at some of the signs indicating the presence of the "Whore of Babylon" already within today's European Union.

Chapter 12

THE SYMBOLISM OF ROME, BABYLON AND REVELATION WITHIN THE E.U.

As one looks at the symbolism within the European Union, Catholic and apocalyptic imagery is seen everywhere.

The European Parliament sits in Strasbourg. For centuries this city was at the heart of the Holy Roman Empire of Charlemagne and the Popes of Rome.

The 12 starred flag of the European Union has nothing at all to do with the member states, as was previously believed by many. When the union was increased to 15 member nations, the EU confirmed that the flag would remain with only 12 stars. Writing in "The European" of 14th-20th December 1995, Allison Parry, European Executive Vice President Woman of Europe Award, Stated "....The 12 starred European Flag was the official emblem of the Council of Europe from 1955 and was adopted by the European Union in 1986. Some say the inspiration came from the halo of the Madonna in Strasbourg Cathedral..." The stained glass window in Strasbourg Cathedral depicts Mary with 12 stars around her head holding the crown of the Holy Roman Empire over a map of Europe.

The flag was unveiled in 1955 on December 11th to coincide with the feast of the Immaculate Conception, a celebration of the *sinless* conception of the Virgin Mary. A belief made canon law in the year 1854. Catholics believe the woman pictured in Rev.12 with 12 stars around her head is the Virgin Mary. In fact if one studies scripture it becomes clear the woman represents the nation of Israel.

In a small booklet entitled "Europe's Star Choice", issued by the European Union and available in most libraries, the creators of the flag state quite clearly how a Catholic seer, St Catherine-Labore of Paris, supposedly had a vision in 1876 in which she saw a flag with 12 stars being taken around the world bringing peace and happiness wherever it went.

Dr Crampton, director of the Flag Institute, stated: "No one can deny that under these symbols Catholics recognise the presence of the infinitely merciful Queen of Peace in Christ." (61).

Several hundred years ago the continent of Europe was dedicated to the Virgin Mary. In the early 1990's the Marian shrine in Gibraltar was restored at the cost of thousands of pounds. At the rededication ceremony Pope John Paul II dedicated the E.U. to the Virgin Mary.

On January 1st 2002, 12 member nations within the E.U. became the first to phase out their centuries old currencies, and collectively use the new European Euro. On the face of the Euro notes one cannot miss the 12 stars of Europe representing the Virgin Mary. The reverse side has various bridges, one bridge per note. What have these bridges to do with the Roman

Catholic Church? The Pope is Pontifex Maximus, which means Chief Bridge Builder, High Priest. He is the bridge between man and God. As such he is indeed an Antichrist, i.e. in the place of Christ. The Bible clearly states there is one mediator (bridge, go-between) between man and God, the man Christ Jesus (1 Tim. 2:5). Not the Pope or Mary, saint or priest. Jesus only. So one side of the notes depicts the 12 stars, representing Mary. The reverse side displays various bridges, representing the Pope.

When one visits the heart of the E.U. the prophetic symbolism continues to present itself. The £8 million Parliament Building in Strasbourg is also known as the "Tower". It was modelled after Pieter Brugel's famous painting of the Tower of Babel. See above.

Some time ago the E.U. published a poster containing the Pieter Bruegel Tower of Babel. (see over) The poster proudly proclaimed "Europe: Many tongues one voice." This is a direct affront to God who in Genesis 11 destroyed the Tower of Babel which had many voices one tongue.

Today the politicians are said to be attempting to "reverse the Babel effect" and make all men unite. Notice the crane in the background of the poster rebuilding the Tower of Babel. In the foreground all men are united in the work of rebuilding Babel. Under the ever watchful eye of Rome the hope is to make all faiths one, as in Babel.

Notice also, the 12 stars on the poster are inverted revealing an occult symbol representing the occult goat of Mendes or Baphomet. (See our DVDs "A Planned Deception" Parts 1 & 2) Once one enters the E.U. parliament building, there is a colossal painting on the dome of a woman riding a beast. In the Parliamentary Offices building PE1 there is a huge painting of a semi-naked woman riding a beast.

Outside of the new Council of Europe building there is a bronze statue of a woman riding a beast (See above). Also when one enters the Diners' Club lounge in the E.U.'s administrative capital in Brussels one is again faced with a picture of the Woman and the Beast.

The image of a woman riding a beast has appeared on EU postage stamps, including the British one issued in 1984 to commemorate the second election to the European Parliament. Notice the woman riding the beast sits on waters as does the woman in Revelation 17. She also sits on 7 waves or hills as predicted by the

Apostle John for the last days before the return of Christ. Predicted 2,000 years ago in Revelation 17. Rome sits on 7 hills and the Catholic Church as heir of the Babylonian religion now based in Rome sits on many waters or people.

The imagery contained within the above picture is pure Babylonian. The little cherubic figure is not so innocent as one might at first be led to believe. The ancient priests of Jupiter (Nimrod) were depicted in the same way as bestowers of the spirit. He is seen accompanying the goddess Europa (Semiramis) who has been abducted by Jupiter (Nimrod) disguised as a bull.

Incidentally, most statues of the Roman gods, once housed in the Pantheon, are now to be found in the Vatican Museum. But one, that of the god Jupiter (Nimrod), is not. It stands in Saint Peters Basilica in Rome. However visitors are informed the huge statue is that of Saint Peter. Millions of pilgrims have kissed the toe of the statue not knowing they are honouring the great god of the pagans, Jupiter or as he was known originally, Nimrod the sun god. Pilgrims to the Vatican are kissing a statue of Nimrod! Friends today you are witnessing the physical fulfilment of prophecies made more than 2,000 years ago. All due to find their fulfilment in a period known as the last days or the end times. Here before your eyes is the evidence.

<u>You live in those days.</u>

If you do not believe the Bible, may I ask just what will it take to make you realise the world you now live in is the very world predicted by the Hebrew prophets,

Jesus Christ and the Apostles? These are facts, not flights of fancy. The very events predicted by the Bible for the "end times" are the events you are witnessing before your eyes. Wake up before it is too late.

Today, the vast majority of European Parliament members are Roman Catholic. Within Europe Roman Catholics outnumber Protestants, 199,000,000 to 61,000,000.

At this time many millions in taxpayers money has been spent on an ecumenical project known as "The soul of Europe." The project's aim is to create understanding between the varying religions within the E U. Eventually they will be drawn under the protective and loving wings of the Vatican. Many are totally unaware we are in grave danger of losing our religious freedom. Soon it could become an offence to preach the Gospel as Evangelicals perceive it. In fact an anti-racism bill has been introduced in the European Parliament that, by its wording, could outlaw those who believe the Bible to be the only revealed word of God.
Soon it may become illegal to say Islam, Catholicism, Mormonism etc. are false religions. But it will not be illegal to accuse Bible believing Christians of being xenophobic and racist.

All faiths are to be viewed as equally valid paths
to God in this coming new world. To say "Jesus is
the *only* way to God" could well be viewed as racist, bigoted and highly inflammatory. Worthy perhaps of imprisonment. Such sentiments will be viewed as divisive and fanatical. As such they will be in direct conflict with the religion of the empire...the Roman

Catholic religion. Even the monarchy in Britain is in danger of losing its centuries old ruling that the throne may only be occupied by a Protestant. A bill has been introduced into Parliament requesting that it no longer be against British law for a Catholic to be on the throne of Great Britain. If it is passed we may revert back to the middle ages when Protestantism was frowned upon and the preaching of the Gospel was outlawed in these Islands.

This is exactly what many believe Rome and her many friends in Brussels would like to see. A Europe where ecumenical Roman Catholicism is the only religion. Where Evangelicalism is outlawed and where the ignorant are kept ignorant and are ruled from behind closed doors by faceless bureaucrats.

As already stated, it has been reported Pope John Paul II would like to see Europe return to the days prior to the Reformation. But many believe his ultimate dream is to see a Europe and a world where Catholicism rules supreme yet is looked upon as the home of all faiths and "men of goodwill." Is that what you want? If not then shun any and every attempt to woo you into ecumenical and European unity.

Britain is heavily involved in this blasphemous empire and our politicians wish our involvement with the rising beast to be even deeper in the coming days. Are we not in desperate need of prayer? The days immediately prior to the return of Christ to the planet are all around us and yet for the most part the watchdog of Britain, the Church, is fast asleep.

We are not awake to the signs of the times. Any who raise their voice are looked upon as divisive and outside of the current "move of the Spirit of God." The Church is "partying" but like Belshazzar in Daniel's time they are blissfully drunk with another spirit, which bares little resemblance to the Holy Spirit revealed in scripture. At the same time the Church seems unaware that the God of Heaven is weighing them and the world in the balances. And they are found wanting. Then Judgement will begin with the house of God. That judgement could be simple yet devastating as God allows the professing "Church" to go its own rebellious way into ever deeper apostasy. Soon the reckoning will come and oh, the cries of anger and anguish as many men and women awake, all to late, to realise they have been sold a false Jesus with a false Gospel and a false spirit offering a false alvation.

Will you not awake to the sight and sound of prophecy fulfilling itself before your eyes? Can you not hear the footsteps of the Messiah as he approaches and lays his hand upon the door latch of history. Ready once again to enter our world only this time in flaming vengeance and justice? Let me repeat the signs of the end predicted in the ancient Hebrew scriptures are all around us. This is not make believe but verifiable fact. May I humbly ask you, dear friend which side are you on? Truth or lies? Christ or Antichrist? The Gospel of Christ and freedom or the Gospel of Rome, spiritual slavery and a harlot One World Religion that will sweep away every spiritual freedom your forefathers bled and died to preserve? Now is the time to stand and speak the uncompromising truth mixed with the heartfelt love of God for a lost and rebellious planet. Now before the door of forgiveness is closed forever and the final judgement of God begins to fall on rebellious humanity.

Chapter 13

THE GREAT FALLING AWAY

How the once great British nation has fallen from being the envy of the civilised world. We once sent missionaries to far off lands with the Gospel. Now we are having to ask missionaries to come to us. Why is this? What caused this catastrophic fall from being a Christian, to a secular, nation? A nation and a Church that is to almost all appearance comatose and unconcerned as the Whore of Babylon and the One World Government rise triumphantly over the ashes of a once great people? As this catastrophe takes hold the "Church" has "Joy showers" or "joy baths" where congregations lie on the floor listening to music and go into hysterical laughter. May God have mercy when He arrives to judge His sleeping labourers.

One of the foremost reasons for the decline of this once great nation is, I believe without doubt, our treatment of God's ancient people the Jews. Every nation or empire that has stood against the Jew has finally suffered as a result. Where are the empires of Babylon, Egypt, Rome, the Catholic Church of the Middle Ages, Nazi Germany and Communist Russia? These once great empires and ideologies turned against the Jew and as a result dived into decline and defeat. God promised Abraham the father of the Jewish people:

"I will bless those that bless you, And I will curse him who curses you"
Gen. 12:3

That promise still stands today as has been evidenced throughout history. God also told the Hebrew prophet Isaiah centuries later *"For the nation and kingdom which will not serve you shall perish, and those nations shall be utterly ruined."* (Isa. 60:12). Although the Isaiah prophecy will yet find its ultimate fulfilment in the future when Christ reigns on Earth from the throne of His physical ancestor King David, we can see even today the veracity and trustworthiness of Gods word to the Jewish people.

After the First World War Great Britain found herself holding control of the land known as Palestine. Originally named Israel, but changed to Palestine by the Romans who decimated the land between 70 and 135 A.D., the land was a barren wilderness with few towns and villages scattered among her wasted hills. Nomadic people traversed the land as, from the late 19th century, a few Jewish settlers attempted to turn malaria infested swamps into places fit for habitation after buying the land from absent Arab landlords. Britain declared this was to be a homeland for those wandering sons and daughters of Abraham. Many did return in answer to centuries of Jewish prayer begging God to allow them, one day, to return to the land of their fathers. In the meantime the Arab nations who had up to this point displayed scant regard for the land demonstrated against the British decision. In an act designed to ease the Arab tension, which many modern day "experts" on the Middle East problem conveniently forget,

Britain sliced 78% of Palestine away from the Jews naming it Trans-Jordan, known today simply as Jordan. The Jews accepted the division. The Arabs did not. They insisted the whole of Palestine was Arab land. Following the Holocaust of the Second World War the U.N. voted in 1947 to grant the creation of the Nation of Israel. Britain had prevented Jewish survivors of Hitler's death camps from entering the land. They even sent some back into the Mediterranean crammed into ships. Some sank. Some ships made it back to Europe where many of these now totally demoralised and helpless people were returned to the very camps from which they had been freed.

Britain did all it could to prevent the return of the Jews to their homeland. God had declared in so many prophecies that in the end times He would bring His ancient people home. Britain blatantly attempted to thwart His plans and purposes for these days. What has been the result? Isaiah's prophecy has come true. Within 50 years Great Britain has slid morally, financially, politically, militarily, spiritually until she is a third rate nation with no empire and a Church that has all but lost its way. Tell me who would have guessed just 50 years ago Britain and her people would have sunk so low in so short a time? Who would have believed that we would be paying our old enemies over £1.25 million pounds every day in order to be part of the European Union? God has indeed handed us over to our enemies as He did rebellious Israel in times past. Why should He not do likewise with Great Britain who once treasured the Bible, but now spurns and ignores its God, its laws, its promises its Messiah and its ancient people the Jews?

Yes, why should He not treat us in like manner? The punishment is greater because we have had the word of God, the Bible, freely within our grasp but failed to read and take on board its message for these climactic days. We ran head on into the plans of God and this is the result.

Much of the "Church" has no love for the Jews let alone the nation of Israel born by a miracle of God in fulfilment of so many ancient prophecies. And it may well be that soon we shall see Israel's greatest ally, the United States go the same way as her government begins to change her attitude in the coming days toward this ancient and God protected people. Not that Israel is perfect by any means. They commit the same sins as the rest of humanity. They need a Saviour, as do all men. But God had promised in Ezek. 36:22 that when He brings them back into the land it will not be for their sake but for the sake and the honour of His name. In fulfilment of His promises. This is one of the main reasons I believe we have deteriorated to such a lamentable state. We have turned against the very people of God. And the majority of the Church has for the most part showed little if any concern. Christians today know virtually nothing about the prophesied end times and their import. They just want to "party in the Spirit." and "Laugh in the Spirit."

And guess who is really laughing?

Satan and the Catholic Church as they watch their own plans for you and I unfold. How are the plans of Satan and the Catholic Church being helped today? By giving the masses, secular and "Church", what they want…..entertainment not education. Keep them dumbed down, happy, ignorant of the true facts about the world in which they are living until it is too late and the doors of spiritual freedom and political democracy slam closed forever behind them. God help us.

Following after the above, I believe the main reason for the blindness and the judgement that is falling on professing Christians, is the appalling fact that the "Post Christian" Church has watered down the word of God. We simply do not believe the Bible is the totally revealed word of God. The Church has called for a re-defining of its beliefs. Instead of confronting sin, the Church has re-defined sin and watered down its affront to God. We don't want to offend minorities who hold different views to the Bible. So we accommodate the sin and offend God Himself. What an incredibly upside down way of thinking this is.

The conscience of the British Church has become so seared and accepting of sin, Bishops from once darkened Africa had to come and cry out against the English Bishops for countenancing sin in the land. But all to no avail. We have turned from the God of our fathers and we are racing toward judgement whilst foolishly believing we are racing toward blessing. We live like the rest of the world and give no lead whatsoever.

A non-Christian friend of mine with whom I was speaking recently asked me "How can we believe what you say about the Bible when the Church keeps changing its stand on so many things?" Sadly I had to agree with her but was able to point her to the One who never changes and His everlasting, unchanging word the Bible. He and His word are our only guides in these dark days.

Also many Christians in the West are virtually indistinguishable from their unchristian neighbours. They may disappear every Sunday morning and midweek evening, but in between their "Holy hour" they watch the same Godless garbage spewed out of the television into their homes and into their minds where it rots the spirit and deadens the spiritual senses. A recent survey revealed that there is no discernible difference between the television programmes watched by Christians and those watched by people who have no faith at all. Shame on us!

The Christian of today purchases and listens to music or watches movies containing many performers whose lifestyles are totally hedonistic and who have no fear of God. The scenes many "Christians watch on video, at the movies or on television would have stunned their parents and grandparents with their depravity and use of foul language. The excuse we hear from "Christians" who watch such awful time wasting material is "Yes I know there is a bit of swearing and a couple of sexual scenes and some violence but overall it is an excellent story."

Imagine viewing such a movie alongside those who died to give you the Gospel and imagine what they would say to you in reply. Not to mention the words you would hear from the Lord Jesus if He were present there with you. But then, He is, isn't He? But can we hear Him anymore? Have we become deaf to His dear voice? The music and the movies of today come complete with lyrics or scenes that just a few years ago would have been banned. Don't we realise the money we pay for their music or videos help contribute toward their continued riotous rebellion against our God? It's high time we began to live and act like the people of God. And that could mean horror of horrors, getting a backbone and changing our life style. Have we forgotten

"Friendship with the world is enmity with God."

You cannot live in Egypt and the Promised Land at the same time. You cannot worship God and yet live a lifestyle His unchanging word flatly condemns. If you do you will follow in the footsteps of Aaron's two sons. You will find yourself in the shoes of King Saul who thought he was doing the right thing by keeping a little of the world and offering it to God when God had already told him he was not to do so. (1 Sam. 15).

You will be discovered in the likeness of all those who believe they can dictate to the Almighty the lifestyle they will live. "I love you Lord but I don't love you that much." Remember if the Bible is true then "Rebellion is as the sin of witchcraft." (1 Sam. 15:32). And let us be clear on this point. Wilfully living your life in direct contrast to the teaching of scripture is rebellion. And rebellion brings judgement. In one form or another it will come and indeed is touching our nation already. Friends it is time to change our lifestyle and get right with God before it is too late.
Many Western Christian women and girls wear the same tight or revealing clothing as the non- believers

next door. Clothing so revealing that just 50 years ago such dress sense would have branded them as possible prostitutes or at least persons of very loose morals. And the real tragedy is we cannot see anything wrong.

We all agree men should control their lustful thoughts, but are you helping your brother to live a holy life when you dress in such a revealing way that he falls prey to Satan's urges? Christian men can dress and act in a provocative way just as well as any woman. We will not escape the master's chastening if we cause our brother or sister to fall into sin. Consider also, what kind of role model are you for younger people? Some businesses have openly admitted to targeting children as young as 7 years old by advertising revealing clothing. They have even advertised thongs for 7 year olds! Children are not children any more. They dress like mini adults with children's minds. May God help them and protect them. What is so wrong in dressing modestly and conducting our life in a holy and set apart manner pleasing to our Heavenly Father? Is it too high a price to pay for the Lord Jesus Christ who bled and died for us? Is it? Is it so difficult a thing to dress, behave and think in a way that is pleasing to Him and not care what the world thinks about us? The world is pressing us into its mould. Its' way of thinking. Morally, as well as spiritually and politically (Rom. 12:1,2). And the world is doomed! Take the words of C.T. Studd who gave away his fortune to take the Gospel to China:

"If Jesus Christ be God and died for me, then no sacrifice can be too great for me to make for Him."

We need to get back to the word of God and obey it.

The Church has left her first love and is in bed with the world. A vast number of "Christians" take on the world's value system and think the way the world thinks. Today's "Christian" rarely stops to ask: "What does the Bible say about this particular issue or that attitude?" We are too concerned with what people would think of us if we became really radical by taking the Bible at face value and followed its teachings about separation from the world yet remaining in the world.

Holiness as presented in the Bible, is a rare thing to see in the Church of today. To be holy means to be separated for and to God. What an honour for the Christian to know you have been called by God to be separated from this doomed world system. This does not mean to take on a better than others attitude or to dress as if we belong in the 19th century. But it does mean we live our lives differently. It means to live life in love with God, wishing for nothing other than to please Him and serve Him in *all* you do. It means to live life in an attitude of not causing our brother or sister to stumble into sin by giving them wrong messages from the way we conduct ourselves or the way we dress. You can dress modestly and look very chic and cool. You do not have to undress or wear overtly tight clothing to look good. We must wake up to the fact that these are the last days before the Lord Jesus Christ returns to earth. All around us we are witnessing a falling away from the truth once delivered to the saints. Do not follow the world view. It is the view of fallen man. Spiritually blinded man. Man in desperate need of the Gospel. Who will stand in these end days and give the truth to a dying planet? Will it be you? Will you dare to stand against the tide of opinion coming from those around you? Will you stand or will you let yourself be swept along with the flood of sin, immorality and apostasy presently pouring like a torrent through our towns, cities and Churches?

Living for God also means reaching out a loving hand to those who have been trapped by the false unscriptural teachings of Rome or any other false religious system. And in so doing, offer them true freedom by introducing them to the God of the Bible and His Son, The Lord Jesus Christ. Again, I believe the main reason for many of the ills seen in today's Church is quite simply, we have neglected our study of the word of God. Many believers do not read the Bible from one week to the next. If they do, the majority live on daily 5 minute readings over breakfast. As a result we have through our ignorance of the word allowed false teachers and so called self appointed "prophets" and "apostles" to woo us off the path of biblical truth. In its place they have given us exciting prophecies and unverifiable testimonies of healing and deliverance mixed with a subtle plea for tolerance of other "brethren" who believe differently to us. They give teachings that have a semblance of scriptural truth but are, in fact, a total distortion of the word of God. And we have swallowed the lie without once checking them out against the word of God.

It is a fact that by reading the Bible for just an hour a day will take the average reader through the entire volume in about 3 or 4 months. I realise we live in a world vastly different from our parents or grandparents. It is a rush, rush world leaving little time to just sit and be quiet. But it can be achieved if we really want to get alone with God for a half an hour or an hour a day to study and pray. And the benefits of spending time alone with your Lord are incalculable. To sit at Jesus' feet for a while, read His word and books written by men who know their Bible will result in you being instructed, informed and *changed*. You will be more aware of false teaching emanating from politicians, church pulpits and from Rome. In years gone by the Catholic Church was looked upon by most denominations as heretical. Today it would be difficult to find a denomination that believes Rome is a false religion. Christians of just 50 years ago would not recognise the majority of Evangelical and Pentecostal Churches we see around us today. Those coming into the Church today appear to believe the Catholic Church has always been acceptable when in fact the very opposite is the truth. But they will never hear this from their leaders. They are on a new crusade. A mission to band the whole of professing Christendom together and take the world for Jesus. Never mind if the Bible warns of a last days falling away from the truth (1Tim. 4:1-5; 2 Tim. 3:1-13; 4:4; 2 Pet. 3:3;). Instead the sheep are told; "Those falling away are those who are not willing to fall in line with the current ecumenical move of the Spirit." "It's not us. Let us all be one. We can overcome our differences." Yes you can. When truth is sacrificed on the altar of expediency.

Chapter 14

THE STARS ARE FALLING BUT THE SON WILL SOON ARISE

Today Evangelical Charismatics have their Popes. Those stars of the church whose word is apparently infallible. If one points out the errors of many of today's shining lights on the Evangelical, Charismatic, Pentecostal stage one is called a liar, a heresy hunter, divider of the brethren and so on. Even when one points out the errors and plays either audios or videos of these "men of God" you would be told as I have been, "The tape has been tampered with." Or "It's not very clear is it." No it is not. Not when you watch it through rose tinted glasses or have your spiritual ears blocked. We are so reluctant to be like the Bereans of Acts 17 in these closing days of history before Christ returns.

The Bereans listened to Paul's words but diligently searched the scriptures to be certain that what he said was in line with the word of God. Today's Christian is too lazy to check out what his leaders say alongside the word of God. He simply wants to be fed. But many do not care what they are being fed as long as it makes them feel good.

Truth has become irrelevant. Like a spoilt child, many Christians want the sweets that rot their teeth but not the medicine that will heal or the meat that will strengthen, the word of God. Today's Christian wants to party and feel good. But he refuses to sit down and truly study the Bible against the teaching of his favourite preacher. Even now I would guess there is someone reading these words incensed that I should have written such things about Benny Hinn and others. But I am only quoting these men.

If the quotes offend you take it up with them, not me.

The ultimate deception is that many of these false leaders are preparing us to return to Rome. That is the destination of much of the Church today. Many Church leaders believe we are having a revival, and are merrily mixing with the Catholic Church. While they and many in their congregations play with the world and are almost indistinguishable from it. This false unbiblical unity and fake spirituality only goes to show how the flame of true biblical Christianity, lit by martyrs such as Latimer, Ridley and a vast host of saints before us, has all but gone out. If we love those inside the Catholic Church we should be lovingly, tenderly praying for them and encouraging them to leave. Instead many are making bleating noises, like lost sheep, as they seek ways to return to the false shepherd of Rome: The Pope. We should be lovingly exposing the false unbiblical teachings of Rome in an effort to save Catholics from following Rome's false Gospel of works equals salvation. We should, with all our heart, seek to rescue them from the emerging Whore of Babylon which will surely soon arise on the world stage. We should be weeping and praying that God will open the eyes of the Pope and other leaders and bring them to true salvation. Instead leaders of major denominations and groups are joining with Rome to "evangelise

Europe and the world."

Just prior to the launch of "Evangelisation 2000" Anglican Charismatic leader, Canon Michael Harper sent a message to the Pope "We are with you for the evangelisation of Europe." Evangelisation to what? A return to Rome?

Even world famous evangelist Billy Graham, it now appears, has fallen for the silk glove of Rome. Billy Graham said the Pope was his pick for "the Man of the Century." Graham appeared on the Phil Donahue show on October 11, 1979, and in discussing Pope Paul II's visit to the U.S.A., said: "I think the American people are looking for a leader, a moral and spiritual leader that believes something. And the Pope does. He didn't mince words on a single subject. As a matter of fact, his subject in Boston was really an evangelistic address in which he asked the people to come to Christ, to give their lives to Christ. I said, 'Thank God, I've got somebody to quote now with some real authority'" (62).

It will very probably shock many Evangelicals to discover the Billy Graham Evangelistic Association held ecumenical Crusades since, at least, the 1950's. Catholic counsellors were present at many Billy Graham crusades. If a person accepted the invitation to come to Christ and went forward to be counselled, one of the first things the counsellor found out is whether you are a Catholic or Protestant. If the enquirer was Catholic, and Catholic counsellors were present their name, address and telephone number were passed on to the Catholic volunteers to follow them up.

Thus someone seeking to come to faith in Christ was at once returned to the superstitions and false teaching of the Roman Catholic Church. All by courtesy of the world's best known evangelist, Billy Graham.

Just prior to the May, 1957 crusade in New York, Dr. Graham said: "We're coming to New York not to clean it up, but to get people to dedicate themselves to God and to send them on to their own Churches--Catholic, Protestant or Jewish" (63).

In an interview with the San Francisco News of Sept. 21, 1957, Graham team member Walter Smyth admitted that seekers at the San Francisco crusade were referred to Catholic Churches. He said, "Even if the penitents are non-Protestant, they are referred to the Church of their choice." San Francisco is a heavily concentrated Roman Catholic City. When Smyth later denied this, the paper stood by its report, and when Graham arrived in town, the paper asked the evangelist himself whether inquirers were sent to Catholic Churches. His answer appeared in the Nov. 11, 1957, issue: "Anyone who makes a decision at our meetings is seen later and referred to a local clergyman, Protestant, Catholic or Jewish."

In his biography Graham writes: "We were concerned to let the Catholic Bishops see that my goal was not to get people to leave their Church; rather, I wanted them to commit their lives to Christ"(64).

Over, you see Billy Graham receiving his honorary doctorate at the Catholic run, Belmont University U.S.A. where he agreed the Gospel he preaches and the

Gospel of Rome are one and the same. This book has covered a lot of the Catholic Church's "Gospel." Is it the same Gospel as the one in which you believe? I write with not a little sadness, either Billy Graham is greatly mislead or he is not the man of God many believe him to be.

In 1962, the Billy Graham Evangelistic Association acquired the printing rights to the classic book by Henry H. Hailley, "Pocket Bible Handbook." Part of the book describes Rome's martyrdom of millions of believers. The special Billy Graham Crusade Edition removed all these references.

At the Milwaukee Billy Graham Crusade in 1979, a Roman Catholic Mass was conducted as part of the follow-up for new converts (F.B.F. News Bulletin, May-June 1986).

In September 1979, The Christian Courier of Milwaukee, Wisconsin, published the following report on the Milwaukee Crusade: "Sister Maureen Hopkins, Director of the Ecumenical and Interfaith Commission of the Milwaukee Roman Catholic Archdiocese, and a liaison member of the Crusade committee, reported that 120 people have volunteered within the Catholic community to help her with the task of contacting each of the 3,500 inquiries. Sr. Maureen received the names and telephone numbers from the Crusade Committee, based upon the inquirer's indication of having a Catholic background on his inquiry card. All 3,500 were immediately invited to a Eucharistic celebration which was held on August 16th at St. Theresa's Church in Milwaukee. The Mass was attended by more than 400 people. The primary purpose for the Mass was to remind the inquirers that their commitments to Christ should be nurtured within the sacramental framework of the Church."

Christianity Today for Sept. 7, 1979, pointed out that almost a year before the Crusade, Graham had sent a team member to conduct a seminar explaining the crusade enterprise for Milwaukee priests and lay workers. As John Ashbrook states "It is a tragedy that 3,500 decision cards were turned over to the Roman Catholic Church, but it is a worse tragedy when you realise that it did not 'just happen". It was planned by the world's best-known evangelist"(65).

That great preacher of the 20th Century, Dr. Martyn Lloyd-Jones said "A Christianity that merely preaches "Come to Christ" or "Come to Jesus" cannot stand before Rome. Probably what that will do ultimately will be to add to the numbers belonging to Rome. People who hold evangelistic campaigns and say, "Are you Roman Catholics? Go back to your Church," are denying New Testament teaching. We must warn them!" (66)

But warning voices, today, are looked upon with disdain, anger and even pity by those engaged in ecumenical outreach. How the times have changed. There are few who believe the words of Dr. Lloyd-Jones today. Those who do are fast becoming products of a bygone age where true biblical exposition was heard on Sundays and Bible study nights. I recently entered a Church one Sunday evening to hear the Gospel or a word from the Bible. What I witnessed was a pastor asking the congregation what they could find in their Bible concerning clouds. God help us.

The late John Wimber, Charismatic founder of the Vineyard Church movement, was ecumenical in his approach to Rome. At one point in a meeting Wimber stepped from the platform where he was preaching and knelt before a Catholic leader, whom he had noticed in the congregation, to humbly beg forgiveness for the Reformation. It was a regular occurrence to see Catholic clergy, nuns etc attend his conferences.

Korean Pastor Paul Yonggi Cho who heads the world's largest Church, was also a key speaker at John Wimber's Sydney, Australia, meeting in 1991, joining hands in that forum with Catholic priests Tom Forrest and Raniero Cantalamessa, and Catholic layman Kevin Ranaghan. Forrest is the priest who said he praises God for purgatory. Cantalamessa was the Papal preacher at the Vatican. Ranaghan claims that the Roman Catholic Church alone contains the fullness of God and truth and that the Pope is the infallible head of all Churches. Cho put his stamp of approval upon these men's heresies by appearing with them in this forum and treating them as of they were true men of God.

It is tragic to realise Billy Graham, Chuck Colson, Bill Bright, Jack Van Impe, James Robison, Pat Robertson, Terry Virgo, Benny Hinn, Paul Crouch and a myriad of other so-called Evangelical leaders and denominations have played footsie with Romanism through ecumenical activities or have become sympathetic with Rome by watering down the stand taken by their predecessors. They are either blind to the horror of Rome's blasphemous errors or they brush them under the carpet in the name of peace and quiet. "Don't disturb me with facts, we are having a revival."

Some of these men may admit Roman Catholicism teaches error, but they do not have the courage of their convictions to make a stand against them. They have betrayed the faith and in doing so they have betrayed their Lord. They have lied to their hearers with assurances that Rome is "Evangelical" and "Charismatic." She is Evangelical in that she is seeking ways to draw those "separated brethren" and the heathen masses into her arms and under her unscriptural doctrine. The Reformation, in the eyes of many Evangelicals, is now viewed as a huge mistake. How blind can we get?

The Reformation lit the torch of the Gospel for many souls who were chained and lost in Rome's dark and infernal dungeons of works and ritual. As for Rome being Charismatic, simply ask a Catholic Charismatic "Can you get to Heaven without confession, attending Mass, obtaining priestly absolution, performing penance and so on, but by simply trusting in the finished work of Christ on the cross?" If they answer "yes" they are no longer true members of the Roman Catholic Church. Because according to Rome all the above and more are necessary to gain a soul's entry into Paradise. Also as I said earlier, simply because someone professes to speak in other tongues is no pass card to true fellowship. What is required by God is an adherence to His word. Yet, I am sad to say, I believe many are so poorly taught the word of God today they cannot tell truth from error. They will be foolishly sucked back into the gaping jaws of Rome and those of us who sound the alarm will be viewed with pity for not going along with the great march toward a "Christian" world brotherhood.

At this point we would do well to let the words of Spurgeon burn into our hearts

"You Protestants who are today flinging away your liberties as dirt-cheap will one day rue the day in which you allowed the old chains to be fitted upon your wrists. Popery fettered and slew our sires, and yet we are making it the national religion."(67)

Today Spurgeon's words have even more prophetic significance than when he uttered them more than a hundred years ago. What would that dear saint say were he to be allowed to return for a moment and view the Christians of Great Britain and America today? A revival is what is needed. But I know of men of God who are suggesting we may have gone too far and judgement is beginning to fall around us. In our politics, in our religion, in our attitudes, God seems to be letting us in the West go the way we wish.

Many in the Church are like rebellious children who will not listen to their parent. God our loving Father, with tears in his eyes may well be saying "go that way if you must." Falling over and laughing like a hyena is not revival. Weeping, crying and returning to the God of our fathers. That is revival. Living holy lives instead of doing your own thing. That is revival. Preaching the true Gospel of sin and Hell and the need of repentance and faith toward a loving a beneficent God who died in order to save us. That is the way to revival. What we are witnessing today is the beginning of what the Bible calls the "falling away", the prophesied end time apostasy due to appear in its awful fullness immediately prior to the appearance of the Antichrist and the return of the Lord Jesus Christ (2Thes. 2:1-4).

On September 11th 2001 the world witnessed the murder of thousands of people by terrorists who flew three airliners into the twin towers of the New York World Trade Centre and into the Pentagon in the U.S.A. Many are beginning to ask "Is this just the beginning as God removes his loving protective hand from the nations that have turned away from him?" Is this the beginning of God's judgement on America and other Western nations that turn against Him, His laws and His ancient people Israel? In America the words "One nation under God" in the American declaration have recently been ruled by law to be unconstitutional.

And will God continue to defend such a nation? Time alone will tell, but in my heart I believe we may well be nearer the end than we think and judgements are beginning to fall as God allows our enemies to run amok among us, as He did with rebellious Israel. We could see worse than the World Trade Centre disaster come upon us as our once Christian nations turn away from the God of our fathers and He allows our enemies to climb over our walls and take us captive into a world of terrorism, war and a New World Order. As things become more desperate and lawless, events, either contrived by the powers that be or events that play into their hands will spiral us toward a One World Government and religion. Ultimately the "One World" lobby will usher forth one leader to bring stability and security to the nations.....Antichrist.

Today an appalling moral, spiritual and judicial weakness is displayed by most world leaders in the face of a terrifying onslaught of lawlessness and rebellion against all authority as governments discard the laws of God which once made them great. At the same time we are witnessing the growing dominance of right wing governments across Europe. Onto this alarming canvas of decadent Western governments, where the Church is so weak and in many cases apostate, we see the religion of Islam on the rise.

This religion is filling a spiritual void in the lives of many men and women.

One person in every 5 on planet Earth is a Muslim. In Europe there are now 32 million Muslims. In Britain and in the United States Islam is now the second largest and the fastest growing religion. In 1951 Britain was home to 5,000 Muslims. Today it is home to more than 2 million. In 2001 alone there were 25,000 converts to Islam in Britain. Islam is now the majority religion in over 45 countries. In those 45 countries their numbers are over 70% of the population.

Throughout the Old Testament God repeatedly warned His people of invasion by those of other beliefs if they continued to flout His laws and go their own way. What gives us in the West the right to believe God will not do likewise to us when we throw out His laws and bring in our own? We repealed the witchcraft law in the 1950's. Homosexual and lesbian acts between consenting adults in private were made permissible in the 1960's. Over the years sexual sin has become the norm. It's not cool to remain a virgin until you marry. This promiscuity has led to an explosion of sexually transmitted diseases. World wide cases of HIV have reached over 42 million. In Britain in 2002 cases rose by 25%.

I was once at a Christian camp meeting in the 1990's. During the night the security guards discovered a large group of teenage Christians "making out" in the surrounding woodland!

Since passing laws making abortion legal the people of the Western nations have murdered millions of children in the womb. God judged the people of the Old Testament for sacrificing their children to their gods. Will God not punish the "Christian" nations who have sacrificed their children to the gods of self interest and selfish ambition? God is a jealous God. When His people rebel He allows them to go their own way for a while. If they will not repent and revert back to His ways the end result is always the same. Judgement. I believe we are now entering the days of judgement. God has allowed us to go our own way and as a result we are reaping what we have sown. That is not saying all Muslims are terrorists. Many have settled in the West and have become model citizens of the countries into which they have integrated.

But along with the peace loving Muslims have come those Muslims who wish for war against the West. Those who believe in waging "Jihad" (holy war) in order to bring down the decadent Western nations and erect an Islamic state in their place. I pray God will not let it go that far, but that He will awaken His Church to the urgency of the hour and send willing labourers into the streets to preach the eternal Gospel. People, who will, by God's mercy and grace, turn many in our Western nations back to the true and living God. I do believe He will let us go only so far. His eternal will for the last days must be fulfilled.

I believe it entirely possible the Muslim and apostate Christian Church will, with other faiths, band together in the coming days. I have no blueprint of how this will be achieved but I know God's eternal word declares the emergence of a prostitute World Church. One who has many lovers from false religions. I believe an unprecedented spiritual and political crisis is looming.
Perhaps caused by extremists acting alone or terrorists unknowingly manipulated by the men of the New World Order. In the face of this coming catastrophe men will cry out for law and order. For safety to walk

the streets and to account all men as brothers. This will be Satan's master stroke. For it is he who has caused the increase of violence and lawlessness. And it will be Satan who introduces the apparent answer to the coming great world dilemma. Antichrist, the World Government and the False Prophet with his One World Religion. Just as Adolph Hitler, that type and shadow of the coming Antichrist, solved the immediate problems of Germany in the 1930's, so at first Antichrist's World Government will bring in measures to solve, or at least alleviate, this coming crisis.

THE MARK OF THE BEAST

The coming crisis, whether it is the rapture of the Church (When Christ according to ancient prophecies snatches all true believers from the earth prior to His judgement), the problems of the Middle East, some terrorist atrocity worse than September 11th, or some other event, real or choreographed, will require a solution. And Satan will cleverly offer one to the world. In order to draw all men together in a brotherhood Anti Christ will bring in a law causing all men to have a mark on their right hand or their forehead (Rev. 13). This will be another masterstroke of Satan. Normally most would balk at a regime requiring everyone to be marked in some way. But I believe it possible the mark will be a form of I.D. introduced to a terror stricken public in order to identify and monitor the whereabouts of all men by satellite or other technical means. "Thus" they will tell you "everyone's whereabouts on the planet can be identified in an instant making terrorism a thing of the past." The suspect would need the mark to buy or sell anything. This in turn would eliminate the need to carry cash or credit cards which can be so easily lost or stolen broken or wiped clean of necessary information. An escaping thief, murderer or terrorist would find it difficult to hide from the ever watching "eye in the sky." It is reported that the children of some politicians and movie stars have already been implanted with a microchip traceable by satellite.

Yet incredibly the bible predicted just such a day 2000 years ago! The world will gladly, blindly receive this satanic lie because they have refused the truth contained and presented in the Bible (2 Thes. 2:9-12). God will allow them to accept the lie over the truth. God will grant mankind what they have always wanted. Freedom from God. Freedom to have their own man made religion where virtually anything is acceptable.

But the price Satan will require for their freedom will be their very souls as, for a short while, he takes over the reins of World Government and a World Religion where all men are brothers and truth is relative. A religion where man can evolve into godhood, fulfil his cosmic, psychic destiny. A religion where any belief is okay providing you accept all others. And it will all be a hoax, a diabolical lie from the pit. In this new world the uniqueness of the Bible and of Jesus Christ will be totally dismissed.

All men may become a Christ. They will say "Christ is not a person but a title. And all men can attain Christhood and godhood." I believe it entirely probable that New Age beliefs will become dominant, with supposed visions of angels, ascended masters such as Jesus, Buddha, Mohamed, Mary and others calling the world into a brotherhood. But these visions will be nothing less than visitations of demons drawing men deeper into the darkness, away from the truth of the Bible.

The events coming upon us will ultimately have their conclusion in the Middle East around the city of Jerusalem when Antichrist finally attacks and subdues Israel. This will trigger the event which true Christians have longed to see. The triumphant return to planet earth of Jesus Christ as He descends from Heaven and fights for His ancient people Israel. With all we see happening around us today, these days, surely, cannot be far distant. (order our DVD "Signs of the End.of the Age") It will be during this time of trouble many discerning Jews and Gentiles will realise Jesus is the true Messiah and the Antichrist is in fact the worst deceiver in the history of the world.

All these events and more are hovering on the world's doorstep at this moment. Oh for one Wesley, one Whitefield, who can show us the way back to the Father's house in these desperate, desperate end times. But Wesley is dead. And so is Whitefield. There is a famine of the word of God today. There are many preachers. But how many tell us we are living in the end times?

How many are aware of the times? How many know of Rome's strategy for a One-World Church? How many warn us to beware of the soft velvet glove being held out by the Vatican? Instead the majority of Church leaders will take many, dancing, spiritually drunken souls, down the flowery road back to Rome.

As we move ever deeper into the final days before the return of the Lord Jesus Christ, Rome will continue to call out to all and sundry who do not know the word of God, to come and join her in her bed of evil on the street that leads to Hell (Proverbs 7).

Much of the professing Bride of Christ, the Church, has been seduced by the siren call of the Roman Catholic Church luring believers onto the rocks of spiritual adultery with Rome. Woe to those who heed her call and dismiss the voice of the Lord. They will eventually bring themselves into bondage under the religion of Rome and the Antichrist world leader.

Although John in his first epistle says there are many Antichrists, he also says there will be one great, final, singular, Antichrist. The Antichrists he describes in 1 John 2:18 are people who backslide from believing in Jesus Christ. How do they do this? 1 John 4:2,3 tell us

"..this is Antichrist he who denies Jesus has come in the flesh."

All thinking people admit Jesus did exist. So "coming in the flesh" does not mean to deny He was ever born. I believe John is saying Antichrist will deny that Jesus was uniquely God come in the flesh. He will deny Jesus had a pre-existence as very God. He will very possibly water it down suggesting we are each divine in our own right. Jesus will become simply another way to God, along with Buddha, Confucius, Mohammed, Joseph Smith et al. Finally Antichrist will desecrate the Temple of God, which I believe will be a newly built Temple in Jerusalem, by proclaiming himself to be "a god"
(2 Thessalonians 2:3,4).

Here is something to ponder when considering the role of the Pope of Rome in these future events. The ancient rabbis believed that a coming evil personage will desecrate a future Temple. The ancients named this coming one "Armillus". What connection could a Pope have with this prophesied evil personage?

Perhaps the sobering fact that the rabbis believed "Armillus" would be connected in some way with a statue of a virgin!

We wait and watch.

The Temple in Jerusalem was the place where the very Spirit of God Himself resided. As the Temple was being destroyed by the Romans in 70 ad. God was actually building another Temple, the Church, in which his Spirit now dwells. As Christians, we are the spiritual Temple of God, for his Spirit dwells in us, praise his wonderful name. Allow me to ask you this question. As Antichrist will enter a physical Temple in Jerusalem, do you not see the spirit of Antichrist already entering the spiritual Temple, the Church?

Antichrist will proclaim himself to be a god, as did the Caesars of Rome.

What do we find in the Church today? Kenneth Copeland of America boldly proclaimed on his "Believers Voice of Victory" programme on God T.V. 29th January 2001 "Let this mind be in Kenneth Copland. That thinks it's not robbery to be called equal with God." Or take the words of Paul Crouch of Trinity Broadcasting Network, "Then we are little gods.

Critics be gone." What do these heretical claims to be gods have to do with Rome? Surely the Roman Catholic Church knows we cannot be gods? In the paper back edition of the Roman Catholic Catechism page 103 we read;

"For the Son of God became man so that we may become God. The Son of God wanting to make us sharers in His divinity, became man, so that He, made man, might make men gods."

The Lord Jesus warned in Matthew 24:4 that in the end times many would come proclaiming themselves to be the Messiah. Incredibly, hardly anyone seems to question the people in prominent Christian positions today who are affirming that very thing. Benny Hinn stated some while ago "When you say I am a Christian you are saying I am Messiah." "Never say 'He is.' Say 'I am, I am, I am.'" (68).

Benny Hinn's words "When you say you are a Christian you are saying "I am Messiah" are not correct. The title "Christian" actually means "one of Christ's" i.e. belonging to Christ. This kind of false teaching, pouring through the gates of the Church, is the spirit of Antichrist. It is coming into the professing Church at such a rate it makes ones head spin. Yet Christians love and applaud these men and others who promote such blasphemy.

The words of the prophet Jeremiah are as relevant today as they were when he spoke to the children of Israel 2,500 years ago, *"The prophets prophesy falsely and my people love it so"* (Jer. 5:30,31). God holds those who promote and support these heretics, responsible for helping to spread the lies of the Antichrist spirit. You have the word of God but you would sooner listen to fanciful stories which have no biblical basis whatsoever.

How do we expect to be greeted by our Lord on His return to the planet? We are so spiritually lazy, we have let these thieves of truth enter our Church. The guard dogs of the Church have lost their teeth and are fast asleep. Burglars have entered the Holy place and are taking the uniqueness of Christ away before our eyes.

To add to our mounting shame, they are in the process of returning us to Rome shackled and dumb, ready for the emergence of a multi-faith religion headed by the Pope. And all the while we are cosily wrapped up in bed unwilling to confront these men who boldly vandalise the Protestant faith. Instead we praise them for their wickedness and have the gall to thank God for them. We applaud them as they walk away, not only with our physical money, but also with the precious gems, the truth of the scriptures, hidden deep in their pockets never to be seen again. In the meantime we roll over and dream of untroubled days and cosy nights, of cotton wool clouds that will carry us away to Heaven in the rapture.

What will we do when the master of the house returns and finds the guard dogs asleep, the gold of truth stolen from the Holy place and many sold forever, by those professing to be His servants, into spiritual slavery?

In the times of the physical Temple in Jerusalem, during the night, the High priest would walk around the

Temple precincts, to ensure the Temple guards were awake and on the lookout for anyone attempting enter unlawfully. If he crept up on them unawares and found them dozing or asleep he would set fire to their white linen uniform. The unfortunate offender would not only be caught sleeping but would have the added embarrassment of having to run naked from the scene of his offence. The Lord Jesus Christ, our Great High Priest, warned

"Behold I am coming as a thief. Blessed is the one watching and keeping his garments, that he does not walk naked, and they may not see his shame"
Rev. 16:15

Friends, many in the Church of Christ are asleep. Burglars have entered the Temple. And the master, our great High priest is coming. Will you be found sleeping? Will you lose your garments? Will your laziness in the things of God be revealed to all? What will be His first words to you? "Well done good and faithful servant" for standing up to and exposing the thieves of truth. Will He praise you among your fellows for having sounded the alarm as false teachers crept into the camp? Or will you hear those dreaded words of condemnation as He exposes your shame in denying Him, befriending His enemies and condemning many to Hell?

Sombre thoughts I know. But we need to face these things now or face them in that awful day when the gaze of the master rests upon us as we stand before Him at His return.

Now, as at no other period since the first appearance of Jesus Christ, we are witnessing biblical prophecies coming to pass at such a rate it is impossible to deny them. What a wonderful time of opportunity for sharing the good news about Jesus Christ to a lost world. But horror of horrors, just when we have, in our hands, these wonderful evidences for proving God and the Bible, at the very moment we should be standing strong in our faith as we await the return of the Lord.

Just when we should be warning lost souls about the prophecies occurring heralding His return, where is the Church?

Where is His bride? Spiritually drunken. Falling over in meetings, barking like dogs, crowing like chickens, laughing like hyenas, partying. We see Christian leaders embarking on voyages of "spiritual discovery", committing spiritual adultery with those of other faiths who deny the very truths these men are supposed to uphold and defend. And all the while Rome gloats and waits for the dawn of a day in which she will be given spiritual rule over most, if not all, the planet. On that day such a darkness will fall across the earth as has not been seen for more than 400 years. Now is the time to stand and be counted. Not tomorrow. Not next year. Now. Silence only condones the evil. As the saying goes

"In order for evil to triumph, good men need do ....nothing".

And you, dear Roman Catholic, may I, in all humility, ask you to please consider the words in this book. We are not against you. In fact we are very much for you to the point of losing old friends in order to save your soul and light the flame of Bible truth. All I ask is that you prayerfully weigh the evidence.

You can be free of your sin. You can know the forgiveness of God and the assurance of Heaven not Purgatory at the end of your life, when you trust in Christ Jesus and Him alone for your salvation. Will you not at the very least agree to look into these things? Be as the Bereans of Acts 17 who, after hearing the teaching of Paul, searched the scriptures daily to see if these things were so. I am no Paul so you should all the more check what I say against the Bible. Let us make a vow this day to turn and follow the Lord of the scriptures. Study His word as never before. See if these things be so.

To those of you with no religious beliefs at all. Will you not test these things to see if they are true?
Eternity is a long time to regret being wrong. Jesus
Christ did come to Earth. He led a completely pure life. He came for one reason. You. He loved you before the earth or the Heavens were formed. He knew your problems. He knew your heartaches. He saw your tears. Yes. But He also witnessed your rebellion against Him. Being totally pure and Holy He can never permit the slightest sin (wrongdoing) in His presence. You are guilty of breaking the laws of God.

This is so serious just one act of lawbreaking will consign you to Hell forever. You can never wash away your guilt. If you park in the wrong spot in town you will be fined. It will make no difference to your sentence if you tell the magistrate "But on that same day I followed the 30 mile an hour limit. I stopped at every crossing." The Magistrate will say "So what? You broke the law." Just so, no matter how many good things you have done the bad cancels them out.

May I ask you have you ever stolen? Yes? No matter how large or small the item was that you stole, your action turned you into a thief. God says thieves will have their place in the lake of fire.

Have you ever looked at a member of the opposite sex and lusted after them? Jesus warned that to do so makes one guilty of adultery in Gods' eyes.

Because the thought is just as much a sin as the physical deed. God sees all. You will not go unpunished. So already with just two of God's laws before us you have been found guilty of being a thieving adulterer. What makes you think God will let you into Heaven?

The fact that you helped with the washing up, gave money to the Church, said prayers, never murdered, means absolutely nothing. You still remain guilty of the above offences. So how do we get right with God? How can we lose our guilt?

Jesus came to Earth for one purpose. To take our punishment. You can know the forgiveness of God without all the rules and regulations of Rome or any other religion. By simply and sincerely turning from your way of life...rebellion against God. By being sorry for the sins you have committed and confessing them to God. By believing that when Jesus Christ died on the cross He did it for you in your place. In some incredible condensed way God poured your punishment upon Jesus as He hung on that Roman cross.

In an amazing act of mercy God treated Jesus on the cross as if He were you in order that He might treat you as if you were Jesus.

Now all you have to do is receive the gift of forgiveness from God and go free.

And that is the best news you will ever hear.

The Bible says in Ephesians 2:8,9

8. *"For by grace you have been saved through faith, and that not of yourselves; it is the gift of God.*
9. Not of works. Lest anyone should boast."

Saved by grace. What is grace? Undeserved mercy. You cannot earn something that is undeserved can you? If you do it is no longer undeserved. You have worked for it. You cannot work for a gift can you? If you do then it is no longer a gift. You have worked for it.

Jesus said in John 6:37 *"...the one that comes to me I will by no means cast out."*

If you would like to be forgiven all your sins you can be…..now.

Friends I realise I am not at all in a position to look down on anyone. I am the most unworthy person I know to be a Christian. I do not deserve one jot of kindness from God. I am no different from many of you. But one day I came to the realisation that Christ died for me. In my place.

All I had to do was repent of my rebellion and receive His FREE gift of forgiveness. I prayed a simple prayer and my life has never been the same. I'm offering you a prayer to pray. It is not magic. It contains no powerful spiritual force. It is a simple prayer that may help you. Or you can ask God's forgiveness in your own way and have Christ Himself come into your heart and life today to help you live the Christian life.

Dear God. I realise I am a sinner. Guilty and condemned. On my way to Hell. But I also understand that Jesus came to Earth to die for me. To take my punishment in order for me to be clean. Forgiven. Lord I accept that when He suffered on the cross He was punished in my place. Thank you so much. Please forgive me my sins. Change me. Clean me. Make me a child of God. I gladly receive you now. Come into my life, Lord Jesus, and be my Saviour Lord and friend. I ask it in your name. Amen.

If you prayed that prayer sincerely, God has heard you.

But now you must live as He wants you to live. Read the Bible, His instruction manual. Start reading the Gospel of John.

<u>Write to me and we will try to put you in touch with others who can help you grow in the Christian life.</u>

Although you may or may not feel any different after praying the above prayer, do not rely on feelings.

Rely on the truth of God's promise. *"For God so loved the world that He gave His only begotten Son, that whoever believes in Him should not perish but have everlasting life."* John 3:16.

That is for you if you mean business with God. You now have everlasting life. Live for Him. You need not fear the coming storm. Whatever happens you have a home in Heaven today. God bless you. But you must mean business with God and turn from your old ways.

To those of you already in the battle for truth, we may be few in number. But we have a mighty God. You may feel alone as did Elijah but there are many of your brothers and sisters out there who have not bowed the knee to ecumenism and the coming world Church. Things may get darker before we see the light of His face. Evil, lawlessness, terrorism and war may increase over the earth but the master is coming. There is a spirit of rebellion and violence against all authority in our streets. Evil is called good and good is looked upon as evil.

Pray the Lord of the harvest that we who live through these times may be counted worthy to bring many souls to the feet of the Messiah in repentance and humility. May we be granted the joy of being part of His last move of witness and conversion before the great and terrible "Day of the Lord" when He arises to shake and judge the earth.

Soldier of Christ, stand ready to defend and to be a witness to the faith and surely His face you will see. Child of the Almighty, stand awake and watchful at your post ready to defend against the coming onslaught of Babylon the Great. Not with steel or bullets but with His eternal word. Stand, stand, stand with the sword of God, His word, ready in your hand. Be skilled in its use until the great High priest, our dearest, the Lord Jesus Christ, arrives with the dawn.

Stand up. The time to stand is…..NOW!

<u>MARANATHA</u>!
The Lord Comes!

Bob Mitchell travels extensively throughout the U.K. and his messages on prophecy and current events have been heard around the world.

To visit the blog please visit
http://www.shofar-ministries.blogspot.co.uk

To purchase a DVD
http://christian-dvd-store.blogspot.co.uk/

To listen to Bob's online interviews with different speakers on many end times subjects:
http://shofar-ministries-radio.blogspot.co.uk/

To invite Bob Mitchell to speak in your area please contact:
shofaruk1@ymail.com

REFERENCES

(1) R.W. Thompson "The Papacy and the Civil Power" (New York 1876) pp. 414 -15.

(2) Carl Bernstein and Marco Politi. "His Holiness." London. Doubleday (division of Transworld Publishers) 1996 inside cover

(3) ibid. pp. 11-12

(4) Edmond Paris, "The Vatican Against Europe". London. Wycliffe Press 1961. Page 45.

(5) Ibid. page 44

(6) John Cornwall, "Hitler's Pope". (London. Viking Group, Penguin Books Ltd.) 1999. Page 114.

(7) Ibid. page 114

(8) Edmond Paris. page 139

(9) ibid. page 163

(10) John Loftus and Mark Aarons. The Secret War Against the Jews. N.Y. St. Martins Griffen, 1994

(11) Edmond Paris. page 200

(12) Ibid. page 209

(13) Statement made by witness Cijordana Friedlender, from the shorthand notes of the Ljubo Milos case, pp. 292-3.

(14) From shorthand notes of the Ljubo Milos case

(15) Edmund Paris. Page 245

(16) Law offices of Jonathan Levy and Thomas Dewey Easton. www. Vaticanbankclaims.com

(17) Edmund Paris. page 272-3

(18) ibid. page 273

(19) Bernard Connolly. The Rotten Heart of Europe. Faber and Faber. 1995 page xvi

(20) B.B.C. "NEWS 24", Dec. 31 2001

(21) Bernard Connolly. The Rotten Heart of Europe. Faber and Faber. 1995 Page viii

(22) Paul Fahy 1997 Understanding Ministries. See also, European Institute of Protestant Studies, website articles by Prof. Arthur Noble

(22) James A. Coriden, T.J. Green, Donald E. Heintschel. Editors. "The Code of Canon Law". (Pauline Press. 1985) Page 86

(24) Austin Flannery, O.P., General Editor, Vatican

Council II: The Concilliar and the Post Concilliar Documents, Revised Edition. (Costello Publishing 1988) Page 380

(25) Available from Berean Call P.O. Box 7019, Bend, Oregon 97708. U.S.A.

(26) Dave Hunt. A Woman Rides the Beast. Harvest House Publishers, Eugene, Oregon 97402. (1994)

(27) Henry White, "The Massacre of St. Bartholomew". London: 1868

(28) Ibid.

(29) Ibid.

(30) Ibid

(31) Dave Hunt. A Woman Rides the Beast. Harvest House Publishers,

(32) Plains Baptist Challenger, June 1984. See http://www.waytolife.org

(33) Mediator Dei. no. 79

(34) Council of Trent. 1545-1563. Session 22 Chapter 2

(35) From Adam Clarke's Commentary on the Bible

(36) Dogmatic Theology for the laity page 262

(37) Council of Trent. 1545-1563. Session VI, Can. 12

(38) The Sunday at Home op. cit. Charge to the Diocese of Liverpool, 1887, reprinted in Charges and Addresses, J.C. Ryle (1903), and Knots Untied, p.505

(39) Salt Lake Tribune, Sat., May 22, 1999

(40) Ibid.

(41) Ibid.

(42) March for Jesus, page 131

(43) Dave Hunt. A Woman Rides the Beast. Page 417, Harvest House Publishers, Eugene, Oregon 97402. (1994)

(44) Signs of the Spirit, Official Report of the Seventh Assembly, ed. M. Cinnamon (Geneva: W.C.C., 1991), pp.38-39.

(45) Geoffrey Chapman. Catechism of the Catholic Church, pocket edition, A Cassell Imprint. Wellington House, 125, Strand, London WC2R 0BB page 197

(46) Geoffrey Chapman. Catechism of the Catholic Church, pocket edition, A Cassell Imprint. Wellington House, 125, Strand, London WC2R 0BB, page 195

(47) Pope Pius XII. Munifcentissimus Deus no. 44. (1950)

(48) Vatican II "Dogmatic Constitution on the Church" no. 58

(49) Pope LEO XIII Adiutricem Populi

(50) Pope Pius IX. Ubi Primum

(51) Herbert J. Pollitt, "The Inter-Faith Movement, The New Age Enters the Church, page 29. (The Banner of Truth Trust 1996)

(52) Pope John Paul II, Crossing The Threshold of Hope" page 221

(53) Bosnian President Alija Izetbegovic from his book "Muslim Declaration"

(54) Croatian President Franjo Tudjman "Wastelands of Historical Reality."

(55) Robert Hutchinson,"Their Kingdom Come" (Transworld Publishers 1997) pages 375- 414

(56) Order our video "The New World Order and You." £11.00 U.K. $28.00 U.S.

(57) Michael de Semlyen, All Roads Lead to Rome? Dorchester House Publications, 1991. page 80

(58) Malachi Martin (an ex-Jesuit priest at the heart of the Vatican), The Keys of this Blood, p142-3.

(59) Carl Bernstein and Marco Politi. "His Holiness" London Doubleday (Division of Transworld Publishers) 1996 inside cover

(60) Mediatrice et Reine, 1973

(61) The Gospel Standard, Feb. 1986

(62) G. Archer Weniger, "Preliminary Considerations for Fundamentalists on the Graham Ecumenical Evangelistic Campaign Scheduled for San Francisco, April 1958

(63) Billy Graham, *Just As I Am*, p. 163

(64) John Ashbrook, New Neutralism II

(65) Dave Hunt. *A Woman Rides the Beast* Eugene, Oregon 97402. (1994) page 414

(66) November 12th, 1876, sermons, 22, 634

.

Printed in Great Britain
by Amazon